TEXAS DEATH ROW

Designed by John A. Langston

Photograph on page 1: Main entrance to Ellis unit

Excerpts from all prisoners' correspondence, interviews,
and essays are used by permission of the authors.

Photographs and documents reproduced on pp. 28, 39, 41,
49, 66, 102, 116, 117(R), 118, and 122 are courtesy of
Texas Department of Criminal Justice.

Library of Congress Cataloging-in-Publication Data

Light, Ken.
    Texas death row / photographs by Ken Light;
    text by Suzanne Donovan.
        p. cm.
    ISBN 0-87805-950-4 (cloth). — ISBN 0-87805-951-2
(pbk.)
        1. Death row—Texas.   2. Death row—Texas—
Pictorial works.   3. Death row inmates—Texas.
4. Death row inmates—Texas—Portraits.
I. Donovan, Suzanne.   II. Title.
HV9475.T4L54   1997
364.6'6'09764—dc20   96-41256
                                        CIP

British Library Cataloging-in-Publication data available.

We dedicate this work to those who speak in faint voices
and to their victims. We can never truly banish from the human community
those we condemn, for they are part of us and we of them.

ACKNOWLEDGMENTS

We are indebted to Wayne Scott, executive director of the Texas Department of Criminal Justice, who allowed us unprecedented access to Death Row. Among the people who were instrumental in opening the prison doors for us and making this project happen are Dorothy Browne, Steve Martin, Warden George Pierson and Warden Bruce Thaler, Captain Billy West, and David Nunnelee.

A number of correctional officers helped to smooth the way and were open about their thoughts concerning this project. They rarely complained during our visits, even though our presence on the Row meant extra work for them. While a few were openly hostile, there were always supportive nods or words from others.

Numerous Death Row prisoners helped pave the way for the taking of the photographs by spreading the word about our project, and we thank them. We would like to recognize all who agreed to be interviewed and who freely offered their insights and perceptions: Andrew, Anibal, Anthony, Billy, Bobby, Bruce, Carl, Dave, David, Emerson, Frank, Glen, George, Harvey, Irineo, James B., James C., James G., James M., Jamie, Jessy, Johnny, Leo, Lester, Michael, Patrick, Richard, Rocky, Thomas, Willie, friends and relatives of the condemned, and family members of the victims of the crimes committed by these men. Sadly, not everyone's photograph or words could be used; in a work such as this, only a small portion of the material can be published.

Special thanks are due Jocelyn Benzakin, who was instrumental in seeing these photographs enter the world, Jimmy Colton at *Newsweek* for his help in first publishing them, and Marcel Saba for his continuing support. Kim Komenich, Michelle Vignes, and Steve Dietz looked at the work as it progressed and gave advice and support. Others who offered encouragement and financial assistance are Lucy and Jim Edwards, Tim Fuller, Eden Harrington, Dick Lavine and Chula Sims, Marynell Maloney, Standish Meacham, Heather Millar and Pete Young, Rick Prinz, Alan Ramo, Naomi Schalit, Professor Mike Tigar, Patrick Wiseman and Wiseman, Durst and Tuddenham, and Dan Wohlfeiler. David Anson shared resources and information. Don Hilliker of the Eastman Kodak Professional Division helped with some of the photographic materials, as did Armando Flores, at Nikon Professional Services, with equipment.

Thanks go to JoAnne Prichard, our editor at the University Press of Mississippi, who was enthusiastic from the beginning, and to our designer, John Langston, who oversaw the production of this book.

To our many friends who put up with our running conversation about Death Row over the last two years, thank you. Our spouses and friends helped us to come to terms with our emotions as we tried to verbalize our feelings about being inside Death Row and to sort through the issues of crime, punishment, and victimization. This book has been a true collaboration between a photographer and a writer. From our first discussions about this project, we gave each other the necessary support to allow it to come to fruition.

We especially thank our spouses.

Over the year that I photographed on the Row, my wife and partner, Melanie, was pregnant. She gave birth to our baby, Allison, in July of 1994. Weeks after the birth, she pushed me out the door and urged me to take my last trip to the Row; for this, I thank her. The process of moving from seeing a life beginning to seeing life being taken was especially powerful for me, and her realization of this and her sharing of insights and thoughts made my work deeper and more connected. Having a partner who understands the impulse behind photography and the challenge of the work, and who can offer wise counsel, has helped move this project to publication.

I thank Brian, who has only known me from the inception of this work, for his understanding and his love, and for believing I could do it even when I wasn't so sure. I am also grateful to my family, whose love and encouragement helped me find the strength to turn a dream into reality.

The impressions and images we offer here are ours alone. We hope this work will open some doors for all of us in our struggle to understand the violence with which we live.

J-23 Wing
Maximum Segregation cell block

6

SHADOW FIGURES
A PORTRAIT OF LIFE ON THE ROW

Suzanne Donovan

I first saw the blocks of cells called Death Row in Texas in December 1993, just after my partner, Ken Light, and I received permission to photograph and interview the men living there. Before I spoke to any of these men, we were given a tour of the Row, the same one most reporters, students, and others are given. I had never seen anything like it—rows of men, in cages, condemned to die. Sweating and feeling shaky, I could barely take in, let alone interpret, what I was seeing. Men sat dumbly behind bars. I heard shouts coming from cells further down the row. I imagined most of the men being crazy or depraved. I learned much later that it is against the rules for prisoners to talk directly to visitors, nor are they supposed to make eye contact.

Feeling conspicuously female standing there in my skirt, I only half heard what the guards were saying. The lack of sunlight made everything feel unnatural. Television sets hanging from the ceiling offered the outside world as a grim tease. We had to chuckle at the incongruity of perennial losers watching ancient reruns of Perry Mason, the television lawyer who never lost a case.

I was choked by the mix of smells and my own fears and uncertainties; I recall even feeling somewhat awed. But overlaying it all was a profound sense of sadness. A palpable depression clung to everything. Even the comment by the captain of Death Row officers—that the guards are as institutionalized as the prisoners—seemed less insightful than dreadfully cynical, albeit on target.

In late 1993 I had written to Andy Collins, then executive director of the Texas Department of Criminal Justice, to propose a photojournalism project about the state's Death Row. I wanted to produce a straightforward, unsentimental view of a place that has been shrouded in mystery, to offer the human face of these men, the pre-dead. We were interested not in individual cases but in creating a portrait of life on the Row. He gave us permission, but it was his deputy at the time, since promoted to director, who really let us in. Wayne Scott is a former corrections officer and was, during a particularly turbulent period, assistant warden at the Ellis I prison (now simply called Ellis), where Death Row is located. He has an unusually open attitude about the

Row, and imposed few formal conditions on our work.

Ken's photography equipment had to be searched when he went in and out of the prison, and he couldn't photograph men being disciplined. At least one officer had to be with Ken at all times, although as time went on some officers allowed him greater access. He was not allowed inside the cells in the high-security wings they call Administrative Segregation. The warden in charge of the Row was always aware of our progress. I interviewed in the visiting room but was allowed unlimited time to talk with anyone I requested, as long as the prisoner agreed, and provided he wasn't in solitary confinement at the time.

The limits were imposed not only by the authorities citing the usual security concerns but also by the prisoners. I'll never forget the incredulous tone of Thomas, one of the first prisoners I met, when I told him that I wanted to learn about his life on the Row, what it was like day to day, how it felt to be simply waiting to die. *"Are you from this country? It's easier to pull down a star than to tell that story."*

There was also the unspoken dividing line of gender, as well as the chasm that exists between those who have committed a violent crime and those who haven't. I often felt men were telling me things they imagined I wanted to hear. On the other hand, my femaleness allowed some men to open up a bit and express some genuine emotions. I was continually struck by how raw, dare I say vulnerable, so many seemed to be just below the layers of mistrust, anger, and violence.

I avoided bringing up the specifics of the condemned men's cases, primarily because our intent was to learn about their lives on the Row, but also because they're constantly warned against such discussions. I assumed these men were guilty, although I know not all of them were the triggermen in the murders that brought them there. Whether this was a reflection of my own cynicism or simply reality, I'm not certain. There are wrongfully convicted men and women on death rows around the country, but we weren't there to uncover the innocent. I knew these men couldn't afford to be totally honest with me about their crimes, and I was intensely aware that Ken and I were forever outsiders there. This is their world.

On the other hand, I never felt self-righteous in relation to the people I interviewed. Many of these men did commit monstrous crimes, and I had some bone-chilling interviews in which men volunteered detailed descriptions of those crimes. Yet while talking with many of them, I was struck more by what we have in common, the fragility of our lives and the potential for violence within all of us. I referred to this privately as my "there but for the grace of God go I" experience, and I often found it hard to talk about what I was seeing and hearing with anyone who hasn't been exposed to this world. Most people don't want to think about how much they share with someone sentenced to die.

I began interviewing the condemned in the visiting room of Texas's Death Row in January 1994, while Ken was photographing life inside. We were ultimately permitted unprecedented access over the next several months to observe, ask questions about, and photograph daily life on the Row.

For me, stepping into the Death Row visiting room was like entering another dimension. I watched lovers and family members trying to connect through the thick steel-laced glass and iron mesh screens separating them. I couldn't help but overhear animated conversations between prisoners and their spiritual advisors or lawyers as I waited for my next interview in that predictable, cinderblock-walled room. The dull linoleum floor was swept constantly, slowly, methodically by prisoners told to keep their eyes down. Soda and snack machines line two of the walls—it's customary to offer a drink or chips when you visit—and against another stands an oversized display case. Built by a prisoner long ago, the case holds Death Row crafts for sale, such as brightly colored bead earrings, clocks to which pictures of deer or other nature scenes have been laminated, and sometimes crocheted blankets or ponchos.

This is a collaborative work. The pictures, as we hoped, tell their own story. They are intimate portraits of daily life on the Row. Some are accompanied by quotations, pieces of letters, or stories sent to us by prisoners I interviewed. Others are paired with institutional records, themselves composites of intake forms, court records, newspaper clippings, and other documents.

We chose Texas not only because of the access granted, but because of its stature among death rows nationally. There is unabashed public support for the death penalty in Texas. Of the three thousand individuals, mostly men, waiting to be executed in this country, typically four hundred or so of them live on Death Row in Texas. The gallery of the condemned here has grown from a single row of cells holding twenty-four men at the old prison in downtown Huntsville in 1977 to six wings of cells (each wing has three levels or "tiers") at Ellis, the maximum security prison several miles outside of town. The six women on Death Row in Texas are held at a women's prison in Gatesville.

While forty states provide for capital punishment, nowhere has it been embraced as enthusiastically as in Texas, with a reported 90 percent public approval rate. No state has executed as many men with more certainty and dispatch—more than one hundred by lethal injection since the death penalty was reinstated in 1976, fully one-third of all executions in the United States.

Despite their enthusiasm for capital punishment, though, most Texans, if asked, couldn't name who was executed when, and aren't aware that thirty-three men died by lethal injection in 1994 and 1995, for instance. Probably many wouldn't care. They are as numb to the state killings as they've become to the extraordinarily high murder rate with which they live. These days, anyone interested has to search the state's newspapers thoroughly for notices of executions.

Texas may be on the cutting edge of a national trend supporting capital punishment. Executions offer the allure of simplicity and completion, or "closure," as it is often described by its advocates. In execution there appears to be the hope of an answer to the senseless rise in murders, even if it is man-by-man justice. But if as a democratic society we want the state to carry out the ultimate punishment—for whatever reasons, from deterrence to unapologetic vengeance—then it is incumbent upon each of us to examine clearly and honestly what we have created. We cannot afford to remain blind to this invisible sector of our society.

The average length of time between conviction and execution in Texas is seven and a half years, but it hasn't been uncommon for an inmate to live on the Row for a decade or more. (This will change eventually, since recently passed state and federal laws governing post-conviction habeas corpus appeals are designed to reduce the time from final conviction to execution.) Each month two to three new men arrive on the Row, or "drive up," as they say, many in their early twenties and, more frequently now, in their late teens.

The image of Death Row as a place of darkness and relentless despair has been created from popular culture and from flimsy media stories. Death Row in Texas has those qualities and many others. But when you scratch below the surface, you get a glimpse of a complex underworld. Nothing is as it appears, or as we on the outside imagine.

It is a world built of concrete, steel, and absolutes—"snitches are rats," as one prisoner put it, and "in here, you got your balls and you got your word." Guards wear gray suits; prisoners wear white. Yet it's a tangle of moral ambiguities. While racial animosity runs deep, Aryan Brothers have been known to make friends with African Warriors. No one can be trusted; still, some men speak of bonding with others in this world as they never could outside, in the free world.

Listening to the prisoners, their guards, various chaplains, the warden, and family members of the condemned, as well as their victims, I discovered a robust if reluctant community. Put simply, Death Row is full of life.

From the town square in Huntsville, signs direct you to several "units" in the surrounding area (in corrections jargon, prisons are units that are managed by the system). This small Baptist town in east Texas is the administrative heart of the largest and most prosperous prison system in the free world—it's a company town where the company happens to be the prison bureaucracy. Some days you can still see prisoners in their white suits cleaning and tending to public properties around town, and, if you hang around for a while, you are likely to hear escape stories from the old-timers. Ex-cons marry prison guards, guards meet and fall in love with one another, and some families have generations of sons and daughters working in the system.

The maximum security prisons known as the Ellis and Estelle units are more than twenty miles northeast of town, down long stretches of two-lane farm-to-market roads. The roads are surrounded by acres of fields; old-timers refer dryly to Ellis as "the farm." Prisoners work the fields as they have for decades, guarded by armed field bosses on horseback.

Estelle is the first stop for newly condemned prisoners; they are showered and de-liced, get haircuts and white suits, and are fingerprinted and photographed. The men under death sentence then go to Ellis for processing—an interview by the classification committee and a physical exam—and are assigned a special Death Row number. Most of them will never leave Ellis again until their scheduled execution, when they take the van ride downtown to the death chamber at "the Walls," the system's oldest prison. Those who either get a rehearing or are called to testify in another trial travel in shackles under tight security.

The majority live out their time in individual cells, five feet by nine feet, equipped with a six-foot bunk, a steel sink, and a toilet. There's no air conditioning. There is no exercise equipment on the Row. The men clean their own cells. They are issued clean pants and a shirt every three days, and underwear, socks, and a towel every day. Showers, a ten-minute daily ritual, are taken alone.

Life on the Row is governed by a blend of regulations, tight security, and round-the-clock surveillance, but there is a surprising amount of flexibility. Though rules exist to cover every circumstance, they may not affect how the system really operates. Control is maintained through a precarious balance of power between the prisoners and their keepers, and determined men will find their way around any regulation. For example, although tobacco products are banned in the Texas prison system, everyone knows this simply means that cigarettes currently sell for five dollars apiece.

It appears that these men have no control

over their lives. To complain to an official, they have to submit a written form, called an I-60. They can't even seal their own letters, since all correspondence going in and out, except to their attorneys, is read. Yet they speak of sharing food, soda, stamps, writing paper, and newspapers through schemes of cooperative passing from cell to cell. Candles aren't allowed, but razor blades, used in making crafts, are okay. Some men tutor the numerous illiterate; some write letters home for those who can't.

Warden George Pierson says the average man on Death Row is between twenty-two and twenty-five years old; recently, more have entered who are in their late teens. Not so long ago, a majority of the men on the Row hadn't served any time in a prison, or "hard time," before being sentenced to die, and many were first-time felony offenders. In the last five years, however, more men are driving up who have been in prison. The average education level is ninth grade. A fair number test in the borderline mentally retarded range. Precious few even knew, before they were caught, that they could be sentenced to death.

New arrivals to Death Row are interviewed by a classification committee. It includes the captain of the Death Row officers, a sergeant, the chief classifications counselor, the warden responsible for overall administration of the Row, and a staff psychiatrist. The intake interview has a standard format that includes family history (is there a brother or father in prison?), educational background, and criminal history. Height, weight, race, age, and any scars, marks, or tattoos are noted. Prisoners are handed the Inmate Orientation Handbook, a book of prison rules,

and are told how to file an I-60. They also get a handout instructing them on how to exercise in a cell.

Prisoners are allowed one two-hour visit per week from a list of people they designate during intake. Visitor lists can't be changed for several months; most men, when they come in, include mothers, sisters, and girlfriends. Often, as the years go by, old friends and even family members (though rarely mothers) drop off, and new friends, met through connections on the Row or prison pen pal programs, are added to the list. It's not terribly unusual to hear of marriages between Death Row prisoners and their female correspondents.

Newcomers live on one of two G wings— high security cells—so they can be observed for at least six months. After that, new inmates are supposed to go back before the classification committee for a review of behavior reports, including what they did at county jail during trial and how they've adjusted to life on the Row (for instance, whether they obey guards, argue with or assault other prisoners, and keep their "house" in order). They are then classified either "Work Capable" or "Ad Seg" (Administrative Segregation). Ad Seg status prisoners are more restricted and have less mobility. They remain in their cells twenty-one hours a day, even for meals, when food trays and a drink are pushed through a slot in the bars.

Classification determines everything, from a man's daily schedule of meals, showering, working, and exercising, to commissary privileges— all of which can be taken away or restricted at any time. Ad Seg men's status is reviewed every six months by the committee, and, while the

rules are spelled out in the inmate handbook, the process boils down to whether or not a man can go along with the system or figure out how to keep from drawing too much attention to himself. Major violations include weapons or drug possession, refusing orders, and, of course, physical assault, but the truth is that prisoners get written up for anything by guards.

Being classified Work Capable is considered a privilege by the system; indeed, Texas is unique in its running of a death row work program. To obtain this status, a man must agree to be evaluated by a prison psychologist, whose report becomes part of his prison record, or jacket. Some men refuse to work because they are so mistrustful or disdainful of the system's psychiatrists. If the committee determines that a prisoner can work, he can opt to work, or he can remain on a G wing locked in his cell twenty-one hours a day, in what is called "lockdown."

Those who choose to can work a regular four-hour shift at the garment factory or at a handful of other jobs; some are barbers or Death Row porters, who help serve food to men in lockdown. They are moved to the H wings, where most of them live in double cells, ten feet by nine feet, with another man. When a prisoner's execution date arrives, however, he has to leave the work program and move to a higher security Ad Seg wing until five days after his stay of execution, if he has received such a stay. For those whose legal cases are active—and there's no rhyme or reason as to which cases are—this becomes a cyclical process as the case winds its way through the chain of courts.

The violent and aggressive—those jacketed as gang members, or who don't follow prison rules, or whom the system deems uncooperative—live on the maximum security J wings. The vast majority of prisoners live in lockdown on either G or J wings. They're allowed out every day for three hours in small groups, to the yard or to the day room, although some men must spend even their rec time alone.

Many men talked about their initial fears in facing Death Row, the "end of the line," as it is often called. Once they were convicted and sentenced to die, most believed they would be executed right away. Almost no one anticipates the months or years of waiting, or how living on the Row will change them. For some, it's a form of torture worse than the final injection of drugs that awaits them.

First Impressions

Willie came onto the Row in July 1994, his first time in any prison. His impish smile and a disarming naiveté made him seem younger than his twenty years. Fresh out of a rural Oklahoma town, he believed the other county jail prisoners when they said he would get shots regularly on the Row to prepare him for the final injection.

When we talked, he had only been there about two weeks. He was still in shock, and was deeply depressed. He had never been in serious trouble before. He said he had gotten mixed up with the wrong crowd, selling drugs. Like others I interviewed, he talked as though he had suddenly found himself in the midst of a murder with no solid explanation as to how or why he had gotten there. He described his disbelief when the verdict was announced.

"The judge, he told me to stand up . . . and when he said, 'You're sentenced to death,' my mind shot somewhere else. I didn't even think about that death penalty. My mind went somewhere else. I heard my sisters and a few friends in the background and they started crying and stuff, and I couldn't even look back. I was just—whoa. I never think, you know, the Death Row? Man, I never even been in a penitentiary, what am I doing here?"

Willie knows his life outside is over. He was in the first of a series of deaths that every man sentenced to die goes through. He just wanted to "get in my own little world." He spent most of his time sleeping, and cut off correspondence with his family, finding even the pictures of his two young children too painful to look at. He talked about slowly coming to terms with the realization that this was where he would die.

"I asked one guard here . . . what it was like. He said, 'Just mind your own business and show some respect and you'll get respect, and you'll be all right.' That's what I been doing so far. . . . When I'm in my cell, mostly I'm covered up and I'm trying to go to sleep. I ain't got nothing to read. I try to sleep as much as I can; got my head covered up. Yeah, that thought keep running through my mind, me on Death Row. I'll be shaving or cutting my hair or something in the mirror, 'Me, I can't believe this, from a small old one-horse town, I'm on Death Row.' Sometimes I refuse to believe it, but it's hard."

Dave came onto the Row in 1991. He had held numerous jobs on the outside, from programming computers to selling stocks to managing a nightclub. He supported the death penalty and voted "law and order" Republican. Because he is educated and painfully soft-spoken, it is difficult to imagine him here. His defense at trial that he "snapped" seems plausible in retrospect. Newspaper accounts of his trial report that, while robbing the club he had previously managed, he forced three employees face down on the ground at gunpoint, tied them up, and senselessly shot one of the young women after attempting to sexually assault her. Dave offered his preconceptions of the Row.

"I had the popular image of Death Row, born of countless movies. Mirrors sticking out of cages, rampant homosexuality . . . a lot of violence on a daily basis. All these men locked up together who have 'nothing to lose,' they're facing the death penalty. Why not kill each other off, why not stab guards for lunch? They're the 'worst of the worst' so why wouldn't they kill each other?"

The Tiers of Death Row

Richard was convicted in 1985 of killing and robbing three people in Houston. According to prison information, two women and a man were stabbed and beaten with a claw hammer in a townhouse in the northwest part of the city. He had met one of the women during the day, had had drinks with her in the townhouse that evening, then later returned, broke in, committed the murders and walked away with $350.

He estimates there were 150 guys when he came onto Death Row in 1986, most of whom he got to know. When I interviewed Richard, he seemed oblivious to the cage in which he sat on the other side of the steel-reinforced glass-and-iron screen separating us. His complexion is that unhealthy prison off-white, and he still carries a hint of Alabama in his talk, although he left there more than a decade ago. Preferring to live on G wing now, he is one of many who willingly give up the relative freedoms offered by the work program to be left alone in his cell. "Am I crazy or am I sane I don't know. I live in my mind a lot, I close myself off. Maybe I'm punishing myself.

"You got three levels of Death Row: you got the dungeon, J-21 and 23, and you got . . . the next level would be something comparable to this [he gestures at the small cage he sits in]—cages—where you're locked up twenty-one hours a day, and then you have the work program. That's the penthouse, where you have freedom to go in and out, recreate when you want to. In turn, you give them four hours of your time. I live on the mid level. 'Voluntary exile' is what I call it. I don't like working for the Man who's gonna kill me. I find the harassment's less—shakedowns, like when you go to work, they got four hours in your house. I consider my stuff the only thing that's private to me."

Since there isn't any privacy—all cells are open for observation, and a shakedown, or search, can occur anytime—the men's property means a great deal to them. They're only allowed a handful of belongings, all of which must be documented with property slips. If a guard sees a prisoner wearing a gold chain, for instance, he can demand to see the slip at any time. If there isn't one, the prisoner loses the chain. The official list of property which prisoners can purchase or receive includes portable radio, wristwatch, electric fan, electric razor, headphones, typewriter, religious medal or cross with a chain, and ring. Legal papers must fit into a regulation-size steel box; spillover from that can be confiscated.

Prisoners spend their time watching TV, reading, writing, listening to the radio, sleeping, and constantly talking. The noise is nonstop—running conversations, gossip, storytelling, jokes and jive, yells at one another or at shows playing on the TV sets. Guys who aren't restricted "piddle," or make crafts that they sell to pay for stamps, extra food from the commissary, and other items. Examples of cross-stitching and drawing, hand-beaded jewelry, and clocks or boxes made painstakingly from toothpick-size sticks glued together in elaborate designs are assembled in these cells and sold to friends and family members outside, as well as to guards. There are at least three newsletters or journals written and produced by prisoners working jointly, and countless personal defense campaigns are run out of this Death Row.

The maximum segregation J wings are distinguished by violent reputation and ultratight security. Prisoners on J-21 and J-23 are escorted to and from their houses by two guards; their hands are cuffed behind their backs, and they are isolated from other prisoners by a Plexiglas shield that runs along ceiling tracks. The shield really protects the guards, who, over the years, have had feces, scalding hot peanut butter, and other things hurled at them through the bars. The shield and additional iron mesh screens covering the bars of J wing cells make these occurrences less likely. A number of men choose to live on J-21 and J-23, saying they prefer the raw honesty of these surroundings.

"Most people on [J-]21, their mentality is the same—we don't sit up and talk to officers all day, we don't see the officers as our 'friends.' If an officer messes over one inmate, everybody feels like he's messed over everybody, right? So it's not uncommon to get the whole wing flooding, setting fires or rejecting the food, and the whole wing's been on lockdown."

"Not uncommon" may be an exaggeration, but Little E tells it like he sees life there. He's lived on both J-21 and J-23 and spent his fair share of time in solitary, his privileges regularly revoked for breaking rules. Everyone can be locked down whenever any one of them tries to escape.

Little E holds onto his Dallas street sense, where he learned to strike first and not wait to get hit. He was just eighteen when he was convicted in 1989 for shooting an employee while robbing a Captain D's Seafood Restaurant in Dallas; he's in his mid-twenties now, a self-described African Warrior. His philosophy is a blend of street savvy and emerging political awareness. He doesn't pretend to be a spokesperson, but his us-vs.-them mentality seems to be more common among the young men coming in now. His fierce pride extends to physical boundaries he draws around his personal space. He talks openly about stabbing or hurting anyone who steps over the line. There are exceptions, but mostly guards are on the other side of the line simply because they're in gray suits.

"I know the guys here [on J wing], they know me; everybody that's been there has been there a while. We have what I would say is a mutual respect. They have gang members on the wing. In fact, the guys there—I wouldn't say they're more violent than anyone else on Death Row because . . . we are all here for a violent crime—

but I would say they're more quick to react than sit back and want to talk about it. They feel like it's understood—you respect me, I'll respect you.

"I feel that guys on Death Row have been manipulated to the point that they don't even know themselves. They can't even relate to, I would say, human instinct. They are content with being disrespected, degraded, humiliated, and so forth. And the individuals on 21 are not content with that. We want to be treated with respect . . . and we will engage in physical confrontations with the system to get that respect. Because we may assault an officer, they say it's crazy. Officers run around here and assault us! They run around and kill us! So I'm saying, if you assault one of them, if you kill one of them, why does that make you crazy? It should make the system just as crazy then."

The garment factory, on the other hand, is the crown jewel of Texas's Death Row. It started as an experiment in 1981, and remains the only prison program in the nation where the entire work force is under a death sentence. Work Capable prisoners are given certain measures of autonomy in return, like being able to dish out their own chow from an aluminum table holding food that's wheeled onto the wings at mealtime, and eating in the day room if they so choose. Once a week they can go to the prison store to buy additional food or other items, if they have money in their prison accounts. In addition, the factory is well ventilated and air-conditioned, which counts for a lot in the heat of east Texas summers, where unbearable humidity combines with temperatures regularly in the high nineties to over a hundred.

For the warden and officers, the work pro-

gram is a useful management tool, offering incentives for good behavior that don't otherwise exist for the condemned. The program is controversial among the prisoners, however, and many see it as divisive. Through the years, the privileges given to those who work have helped to create a kind of class system on the Row.

James B. has been on the Row since 1985 and, like most who have been there a while, has spent time both in Ad Seg and on the work program. He gave his reasons for choosing to work. "You're on your own in here. You got to try to make it as best as you can for yourself, and for whatever . . . personal peace or status they find for themselves by being in lockdown, that's worth it for them. I never found it to be meaning that much.

"There's a part of me not comfortable working for the state system, especially making officers' clothing. On the other hand, work is work, labor is labor, time is time. Whatever I do to pass the time . . . for the other privileges I have, it's worth it for me. I'll eat a lot of shit working for the system for my mother to not visit me in those cages."

The most valued privilege garment factory workers discussed was the ability to walk unencumbered, without handcuffs, into the visiting room and to sit in a freestanding chair. The vast majority said they chose work not only because it breaks up the unrelenting grind of daily life on the Row, but because it means they are not forced to sit in a separate cage while visiting family and friends. Some talked about feeling humiliated by the guards who escort them to the cage, then unlock the handcuffs through a slot in the door only after they're safely locked

inside. Others said it was too disturbing for their mothers, relatives, wives, or girlfriends. Ad Seg prisoners are not only escorted in handcuffs but also strip-searched before and after every visit.

"Nothing Really Changes . . ."

Life on the Row is by all accounts excruciatingly boring, punctuated by the high anxiety and tensions produced by an impending execution. Daily life is scheduled on a twenty-four-hour basis by the captain who oversees three guard shifts a day—for some tiers, breakfast is served as early as 3:30 A.M., and for others it's 5:30, in order to even out the guards' workload. Televisions come on at 7:00 A.M. and play continuously until 10:00 P.M., later on the weekends. Soap operas, sports, and the nightly news are popular, but the next day's programs are supposedly chosen by a majority vote of the tiers each evening. The reality is that on some wings even this process is controlled by a handful of men.

Texas's Death Row is still dominated by physical force, though the raw brutality found there in former days has diminished. I heard stories of prisoners stabbing other prisoners for violations of "honor" or debt, of prisoners stabbing guards, of guards hurting and taunting prisoners. Gambling and dealing in various types of contraband, which can mean anything from a book to tobacco or stronger substances, is part of daily life. Tear gas is sometimes used to get men out of their cells or the day room, and special teams of guards periodically discipline some prisoners. Officers' use of force is supposed to be videotaped so there can be no dispute over what occurs; in some cases, officers have been investigated and reprimanded for stepping over the line.

There is rape, of course. Physical contact visits, which would allow kissing, hugging, or otherwise touching wives, children, or other family members, are not permitted for Death Row prisoners, and physical contact on the Row is discouraged. But the opportunities for rape and physical assaults are actually fewer than in the rest of the maximum security prison, since the men on Death Row are so restricted and are constantly watched. Seasoned convicts often call it the "safest place in prison."

For those facing the certainty of death at an unspecified future date, time can take on a physical quality. James described his experience of it. "Well, for me personally, when you go through life out there, time is like air to you. You breathe it in and you breathe it out; it passes through you, and you sort of pass through time. But when you're here and it's final . . . time doesn't go anywhere. It comes and it stops. It builds up inside, and it's actually like a weight after a while. Ten years weighs an awful lot. It just builds up, and there's times in the morning when . . . you almost literally feel it crushing you when you wake up and you have to look around and see the same things in here and you're in the same cell and doing the same things that you did years ago, and nothing's going to change."

The daily routine of meals, shower, work, and rec time seems to offer some men a sense of normality, or at least predictability, in an environment where they are otherwise totally at the mercy of forces and individuals outside their control.

Dave gets up every morning at 5:30 so that he has some quiet time alone, before the TV sets come on. Because of his Work Capable status, he has the freedom to dish out his own breakfast. Before his shift at the factory, he's pat-searched. He works four hours, then is strip-searched on the way out to make sure he's not carrying scissors or pieces of the gray cloth used to make guards' pants (word has it that a man tried to escape once after sewing together pilfered fabric to make a gray uniform). Three days a week Dave exercises in the day room or outside with a rolled-up mattress or whatever else he can use as weights. He showers and gets his last meal of the day between 3:00 and 4:00 P.M.

The subject of time, with its corollaries hope and fear, is a thread running through conversations with these men: how to spend time, how it crushes those who let it, how it feels to wait to be executed.

Little E reflects on his daily life on one of the J wings. "See, you don't actually think about it on a day-to-day basis. You come to terms with the reality that you are here on Death Row, and I can only share my sentiment . . . You have no power over leaving and coming. You just somehow maintain. Once you accept that you can't go nowhere, that you're here for one purpose . . . you understand. You see individuals two cells down from you that have been executed. That realization sets in. You think of how you want to leave, or how you want to go home, or about your grandma. You never sit down and say, 'What am I going to do this day, or how am I gonna make it, or what's going to pull me through this day?' You know the routine. You know you're going outside for three hours, you

know you're going to watch TV. Nothing really changes—the atmosphere doesn't really change. It's like you're stuck in time."

James expressed the contradictory nature of hope for him, the tension of knowing he's going to be executed in combination with the will to survive. "Hope is something I really can't afford in here. Hope will kill you—for some people it's the only thing that keeps 'em going. There's . . . a lot of hope in here, so I'm not speaking for most people, maybe even one person, you know, but for me hope's like torture. If I think about hope, then I dwell on 'what if,' and if I dwell on 'what if' I start wanting things I know I can't have. For me, the ability to lose hope, to give it up, has been a real liberating thing."

Members of the public who even think about these men generally remember them as they were portrayed when they were caught, or at trial. The death sentence in essence pronounces these men incapable of change, irredeemable, and unfit to live. Once convicted, they become shadow figures, their images frozen in a media frame. But no one is truly suspended in time. Many of the condemned change dramatically while they are there, some for the better, some for the worse. Other than family and friends of these men, the one group intensely aware of how they change on the Row is family members of their victims. This is another way in which the survivors' lives become unintentionally yet inextricably bound with the condemned, as the survivors track the months and years "their" inmates spend on the Row. Indeed, for death penalty advocates, the fact that these men change is all the more reason to push for executions to take place as soon as possible after sentencing.

There are notable exceptions, but the overwhelming majority of individuals sentenced to die are young men, in their late teens and early twenties. A number of them learn more about themselves while waiting to die than they did in all the years they were free. As one prisoner said, "All we have to talk about is our past," and many spend countless hours trying to make sense of what brought them to Death Row. Some teach themselves to read and write with the help of other prisoners, and take the GED tests to obtain a high school equivalency diploma. Still others, who perhaps came onto the Row as borderline personalities, step over the line into insanity. A few commit suicide. Some become more violent.

Who Are the Condemned?

The men of Death Row are disproportionately poor, uneducated, and African-American compared to the rest of the population (although in absolute numbers, the majority is Caucasian). Though they include former police officers, lawyers, businessmen, and even prison guards, mostly they were laborers of one sort or another. Many men I interviewed were high when they committed their crimes, and their stories of alcohol and drug habits are staggering. Whatever their lives or professions were outside this setting, once on the Row they're stuck with the same fate, and it affects each individual uniquely. Some guys describe it as the great equalizer—everyone's in white suits—but the overarching sense is one of deep isolation. Each man lives this experience privately.

Jessy is in his mid-twenties now. Built with a small but sturdy frame, he has an intensity about him that belies his bewilderment about his life. He is still trying to figure out how he became inmate #999008 in 1991 at the age of nineteen.

His prison biography reads like one more horrific newspaper crime story. He was convicted of the robbery and murder of a twenty-eight-year-old Taco Bell manager in Irving, near Dallas. His codefendant, Jerome Green, was an employee of the fast food restaurant. Two other Taco Bell employees, the manager, and a friend of one of the workers who happened to be in the parking lot at the time and witnessed the robbery were all forced into a walk-in freezer and shot. Jessy and Jerome were caught and arrested leaving the scene. Jerome got a fifty-year sentence for murder. Jessy, with no prior prison record, got the death penalty.

Jessy spends most of his time alone now. Since he has attempted to escape and has fought with the guards, almost all of his privileges have been revoked. He lives on J-21, forced even to exercise by himself in a single-man rec yard.

There seem to be only tenuous threads connecting Jessy's past with his life now and certainly with his future. As happens with a number of men, over the passing years his family wrote and visited less frequently. Without the contacts of family, lovers and friends from the outside, his former life and identity are fading into a mixture of memories, dreams, and what-ifs.

"It's hard to even think about. It's hard to remember. You think about things that could have been—bring up memories that you wish, things about how you wish it could have been. And it gets to the point where you almost forget everything out there, everything that ever happened to you. I know like me, I try to forget everything that ever happened out there. It's almost like those things, those times, places, were dreams that never really happened.

"Sometimes I'll just be sitting in my cell and I'll look in the mirror and just look and, well, just try to see if I can see the difference. Just what I got in my mind, or what I'm thinking. I don't know what kind of expression I could use to describe it. It's kind of scary. 'Cause, you know, I look in the mirror and I see somebody that doesn't look familiar to me."

Since he came to Death Row more than ten years ago, Mariano has earned his GED and become a barber, then a porter, on the Row, and now, in his late fifties, believes he could learn to do almost anything. By his own admission, on the outside he was a hard and unyielding man who couldn't accept others for what they were. He disciplined his own children harshly, trying to instill in them the same traditional values with which he had grown up as a farm worker in south Texas.

He started picking cotton at nine and had to leave school a few years later to help support his family. He married young and through the years built a successful small business with his brothers. It wasn't until he went to Death Row after attempting unsuccessfully to kill his wife for having an affair with a younger man—he was convicted of killing the three other people who were asleep in the man's house that night—that he found time for his own education and to reflect on his life.

"I have learned a lot of things in here. I have been around people a long, long time, the same people—they [the authorities] don't move you around as much. So you learn about other people, and you learn how to get along with people more than what you do out there. I learned how to get along with people a lot better, and in that I see my sons, because I was always real hard on my sons. I was always trying to make them do things the way I wanted them to be done, and that is not the right way for me, not anymore . . . I have learned to respect other people's ways.

"While I have been here I have tried to see back what I could have done different. This place helps you think about these things. Not because I have the death sentence—and it is not that I am a brave person, that I don't care if they kill me. I do care. I don't want to die in here. But you have a lot of time to yourself. This place has made me see different ways that I could have lived my life."

Harvey came onto the Row at age eighteen, a functional illiterate from the ghetto who says his world growing up was as large as the block on which he lived. He spends little time watching TV, preferring to read and write extensively. His own life is an example of how men can and do change; in a perverse twist, his universe expanded as a result of his educating himself on Death Row. "I think all people are redeemable. There's something about the human spirit that's resilient. I look at all of us here as men who are out in the water without life support systems. But some of us are closer to shore than others and therefore some are more easily retrievable than others, but the one who is furthest out, he too or she too is retrievable. But someone has to care. Someone has to care."

Execution Legends and Rituals

Legal appeals for some men have taken years; the cases of others, mostly recent arrivals, are moving rapidly through the courts. There are no simple explanations for the discrepancies. But a sense of public urgency emerged in the 1990s over the amount of time appeals can take, and, in Texas, it erupted into a divisive issue. What the political debate over laws governing capital murder trials and appeals never acknowledges is the arbitrary nature of the criminal justice system or the flaws in death penalty schemes.

In Texas, execution dates are set in each case by the presiding district court judge. There's no oversight and no statewide method or rationality for setting these dates, leading to a situation in which, in some months, twenty or more dates are on the calendar. In a state with 254 counties and a strong tradition of local prosecutorial discretion, there's a great deal of variety in decisions about which capital murders will even be tried as death penalty cases. Add to that a paucity of state resources devoted to defending indigent clients, and appeals court reviews of death penalty convictions become critical to ensure fairness and an even administration of justice throughout the state.

The importance of a thorough review of these convictions is underscored by the reversals and releases that do occur. Although rare, they offer proof that we cannot rely wholeheartedly upon convictions—53 individuals have been released from death rows around the country, while just over 250 people have been executed since 1976.

The effect of these statistics on the Row is to keep hope painfully alive. Virtually everyone there believes he has a chance (or at least says so), that the issues raised in his appeal just might be the ones to convince a judge to grant him another hearing. It's also clear to anyone who closely examines case law—and many men do on Death Row—that the same legal issues presented over and over again have indeed produced different results through the years at different stages of appeals and under different judges. There simply is no rationality to the system.

Because the conviction and appeals processes appear to be random and arbitrary, and because the men on the Row typically don't have solid information about their cases, explanations infused with superstition about the order of executions have evolved.

Many men believe the Death Row number assigned each prisoner indicates execution order—the lower the number, the more likely you are to get killed. A variation on this is that when someone with a number near yours gets a date, you soon will, too. The truth is that, since men with low numbers have been there the longest, some anecdotal evidence supports this theory. But judges don't set execution dates by prison numbers.

Some prisoners say a man is more likely to get executed if he's on the work program than if he's in Ad Seg, though this idea may be primarily inspired by internal jealousies felt by one group toward another, with the resulting rationalizations. There are also stories of guards having parties before or during executions and of body parts being sold by the system to medical researchers after executions.

The stories and beliefs are inadvertently supported by the ritualistic way in which the system carries out executions. Every step leading to the final injection is followed, even when the authorities know a court stay is about to be issued or has been issued to halt the execution. The steps are spelled out in detail in a prison manual, including the precise roles played by the warden and chaplain (an outside contractor), as well as by the technicians administering the poison and the doctor who pronounces death. The technicians and the doctor remain anonymous.

Thirty-six hours before the appointed time, the man is moved with a few personal effects, like toiletries and writing paper, to the Death Watch cell for observation. He's told to write his will. The "execution summary" is filled out by the warden at Ellis and then passed along to the warden at the Walls prison, where the death chamber is located.

The prisoner is asked what he wants for a final meal, what color outfit he wishes to wear, and who should be on a final visiting list. An inventory of his property is taken, and he is asked to whom it, as well as any money in his prison account, should be distributed. He is also asked if he wishes to donate his body to the prison medical facility in Galveston or if next of kin will claim the body. The poorest, and the men without family, are buried in the Joe Byrd cemetery, their graves marked only by a simple white cross inscribed with their prison number.

Twenty-four hours before the scheduled exe-

cution, the condemned man is taken in shackles to the Walls in a prison van by secret route. Officially called the Huntsville Unit, the Walls prison is a brick fortress set right downtown. Older residents like to say they always knew when an execution occurred because the town's lights dimmed. Before 1976, execution in Texas was by electric chair, and, until 1995, the killings took place after midnight. "Old Sparky," the chair, is the most popular display in the private storefront prison museum on the town square—like most of the items there, it was made years ago by prisoners.

Every movement the prisoner makes in his final hours is observed and logged in excruciating detail by officers, first every thirty minutes, then in fifteen-minute intervals: "talking to Chp . . . sitting—watching TV . . . I/M to Seg Office for Incomplete Phone Call . . . I/M lying on bunk . . ."

Slots designated for witnesses include five media representatives, family or friends of the condemned and, because of a policy change in 1995, up to five members of the victim's family. The warden at Walls decides who will actually witness each execution.

At this time the prisoner is entitled to longer visits, and is allowed to call family members and speak to his lawyer. Those who have a brother in the maximum security Ellis prison may be allowed a final visit. Many men take a shower, brush their teeth, and put on clean clothes before they're taken to the gurney.

Richard discussed how he felt going through these motions when everyone knew the court had ordered a stay of execution. "That's their

little thing—it works. You know, even though I knew, it still penetrates. It's really a lonely feeling.

"It's not right. 'Course I don't want anybody's sympathy. But this situation here, this ain't human. There is a certain element of torture. I don't know anybody in here that had a case where they tortured their victim five or six years before they actually took their life. Yeah, there is torture.

"I learned something the other day when I was over on Death Watch. I didn't know this: you're here for so many years and they don't give you a choice—what to eat, what to wear—and then in your final hour, they give you a choice! 'What do you want to eat? What do you want to wear before we kill you?' And I asked the captain, I said, 'What do you mean what do I want to wear?' He says, 'What color?' 'Well, does it matter what color I'm gonna wear?' 'No, it don't matter to me, but they want to know.' White. I been wearing white eight and a half years. It's strange. They give you a choice in your final hour."

On my last tour of the Row, it was lunch time, and the smell of fried fat was in the air. This time around, the five-foot-by-nine-foot cages the men call their houses seemed more real to me. Guards and prisoner porters gave trays of chicken, potatoes, and cornbread to the men in their cells. I was embarrassed to watch. I thought about how several men had told me that they felt like animals in a zoo when outsiders strolled through on tours. But the place no longer appeared so alien to me, and I was struck by how anything can seem normal after a while.

There's no hiding on the Row. I studiously avoided making eye contact with a man we caught by surprise pissing in his toilet bowl. Several men were curled up in the fetal position asleep on their steel bunks, even though it was 11:00 A.M. and a bit of sunlight streaked through the steel-laced windows on the other side of the run. I saw a forty-some-year-old man who was dying of cancer sitting alone on a bare bunk holding a cup, just staring at a wall in the observation cell usually reserved for condemned men before they go to the Walls.

I didn't get the specific answers I wanted—who are these men? What have we created in sanctioning the death penalty, and who is it serving? I recall vividly one man saying to me early on, "The system is mad. Nothing is being solved here. There are no answers here."

Death Row offers society the illusion of finality in the service of justice. It is the "end of the line," yet the ripple effects of each execution reach out and move through us silently, like sound waves. A man takes a life, and we demand that, under specific circumstances, his life be sacrificed in return. When all the legal and political arguments are pushed aside, it seems so basic—a clean trade. We crave simplicity in executing justice. But there is nothing simple about what we have created in the ritual of executing men.

Those whom we would banish from society or from the human community itself often speak in too faint a voice to be heard above society's demand for punishment. It is the particular role of courts to hear these voices, for the Constitution declares that the majoritarian chorus may not alone dictate the conditions of social life.

William Brennan, U.S. Supreme Court Justice,
in his dissenting opinion in *McCleskey* v. *Kemp (1987)*

Night view of H wing cell block

Entering G wing
Administrative Segregation cell block

Looking down the Row
Administrative Segregation cell block

Three tiers
Work Capable cell block

Strip search
"Shakedown room" of visiting area

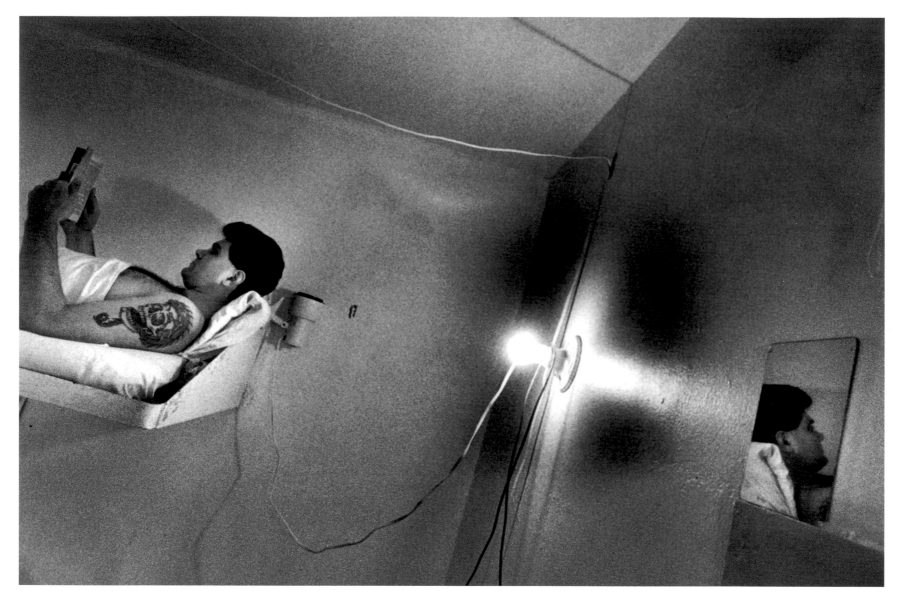

Todd Willingham on his bunk
Work Capable cell block

Bobby Hines, twenty-one years old
H-18 wing, Work Capable cell block

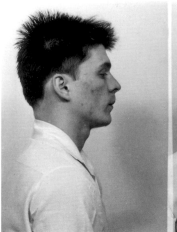

Name: _____Robert Wallace West, Jr._____   D.R.# _____731_____

DOB: _12_/ _12_/ _61_   Received: ___2_/ _3_/ _83___   Age: _____21_____ (when rec'c

County: ___Harris_____   Date of Offense: ___8_/ _24_/ _82_

Age at time of offense: ___20_____   Race: ___white___   Height: ___5-10____

Weight: __139_____ Eyes: _hazel__   Hair: _brown_____

Native County: __Duval_____   State: ___Florida_____

Prior Occupation: ___student_____   Education level: _8 years (GED)___

Prior prison record:

___No TDC record, but in April 1981, West was given a 13-month prison term____

___in Florida for grand theft. Records also indicate he served a prison term____

___in Illinois for burglary and was discharged in 1979._____

_____

Summary: Convicted in slaying of 22-year-old DeAnn Klaus at the Memorial
Park Hotel on Waugh Drive in Houston. Klaus, who lived and worked
as a waitress at the hotel, was strangled with a belt and pillow-
case and then beaten and stabbed with a wooden club after West
broke into her room, stripped her of her clothes, and tied her up.
West, who was also staying at the motel, told police he killed
the woman because he believed she was indirectly responsible for
the death of one of his friends. Other residents and guests of
the hotel saw West leaving the woman's room covered with blood.
He was arrested at the scene about 30 minutes after Klaus' body
was found with the splintered piece of wood still embedded in her
back.

Co-Defendants: __None_____

_____

Race of Victim(s): ___Unknown_____

_____

28

DEATH DAY

I was raised in a small town called Lockport, Illinois, a middle class town 36 miles SW of Chicago. When you came in from any direction there was the "Welcome to Lockport. Home of the Lockport Porters" sign. Then it said "Population 10,000". Around that stuff they of course had the VFW, local Lions Club and a few other middle class organizations, but it was the "10,000" that had me thinking because I couldn't figure out where they hid the other 5,000 or so. While I was growing up there I think I saw everybody in the town at least a dozen times or so, some a lot more than I really wanted to and others a lot less, but nowhere in my mind did I ever think there were 10,000 people there.

My childhood was as American Pie as one could get, Father worked, Mother made everything function, sister went to college when I was real young and set a standard that I could never follow and around that I was the classic fuck-up. At least in retrospect, where you end up in life always predicates exactly how good or how bad you were and in light of that I was a brat and a bully.

I was in the Cub Scouts, played Pee-Wee league baseball, Little League and Park District baseball. I also ditched school to go fishing, drinking and smoking weed with my friends. Those things, for what its worth, made me a bad guy, a poster child for the saying "We are the people our parents warned us about." To me, of course, that was some insane shit cause I was only guilty of consensual crimes and I still to this day feel that those things are nobody else's business.

I could go on here for hours telling childhood stories, vacations we went on with me bouncing around in the back seat, and the thousand or so journeys me and my buddies went on in order to explore the town and its outskirts, but I'd just be rambling and keeping myself away from the reality of the present.

I'm no longer a Cub Scout even though I have a few pictures of myself in that little uniform to prove that I was. Right now I am 20 years and 1,600 miles away from Lockport and neither nothing or nobody remains the same from when I left. You can never go back home.

Right now I'm sitting on the Administrative Segregation cellblock J-21 here on Texas' death row. I say it like that, something you already know, because there are days that my being here is a lot more real than others. July, 17th, 1995. Its been about a week and a half since they moved me back down here to the 1st tier in 6 cell. I occupied this cell for 9 years before getting rolled out of it back in February and taken to solitary. Since then they put two other men in this cell, both of their stays were short lived and both of them were, ironically, from Chicago. The last one's stay got cut short by the Captain, per my request, moving me back "home". In 5 cell, beside me, they put David "Bob-a-Long" Gibbs, a man that had lived in 8 cell and recreated in my recreation group for the last 6½ years. A few years ago Bob-a-Long lived in 8 cell, Dusty in 7, me in 6 and Cowboy in 5. Cowboy, Dusty and I lived here together for the last decade, then Cowboy got carted off in the middle of the night and murdered, snatching a big chunk of care out of me in the process, and then in November of 94 they did the same to Dusty, and that void still ain't began to heal. Now its Bob-a-Longs turn. This date for tonight at 12:01 am was set for him about 5½ months ago, a date that we sat and watched come a-slowly-creepin'. It ain't like none of us haven't been there before, we've all experienced these execution dates, the counting of days and the anticipation of the un-known feel of death, but having a time and a place set aside for the state to kill you is one of those things that you can just never get used to so the ambiguous ever changing feelings wreck your ass every time. The last 24 hours are a real bitch, thoughts get weirder, the day takes on an un-explainable pall, a taste of surrealism, and you know, no matter what other name they use, that you're in a death camp. DEATH CAMP'S IN AMERICA!

Today we talked, Bob-a-Long and I, exercising the gallows humor that keeps us from going insane and smoking the smokes we aren't supposed to have. In that time I recognized how long this day has been so far with the morning and afternoon slowly coming together and stretching into the hot part of the day. Through the small hole in the wall we peeked while we talked, looking to see if any cracks appeared in the others facial armor, those cracks that come when you get to succumbing to the inevitable goodbye's.

At 5:00 pm they came and got him to go make an attorneys phone call, going to listen to a benevolent stranger tell him whether or not he did enough to win him a stay in the courts. The Ad Seg (Administrative Segregation) office is across the hall from this cellblock but when you're walking to hear your fate those 30 or so steps each induce a different thought that makes the walk a long one.

At 5:20 pm he came back, the big, steel 3 key opening the solid steel door at the front of the cellblock and allowing the noise from within to mingle with the noise from the main hall, then the outer is silenced by the resounding bang of all that steel being closed. "Abandon All Hope ye who enter here".

Stepping in front of my cell he said "I got a stay".

The day still feels like a dream, emotions stretched to their limit, a physically exhausting process that snatches energy and elements of your humanity one piece at a time. There is no rest for the weary though, while my heart is celebrating this momentary victory my fingers are tapping out words on this machine because I don't believe every saying that I hear. I will go back home.

Robert West #731
DEATH ROW
Ellis 1 Unit
Huntsville, TX
77343-0001

Bobby West with his Cub Scout picture
J-21 wing, Maximum Segregation cell block

Convict with handmade Last Supper clock
Administrative Segregation cell block

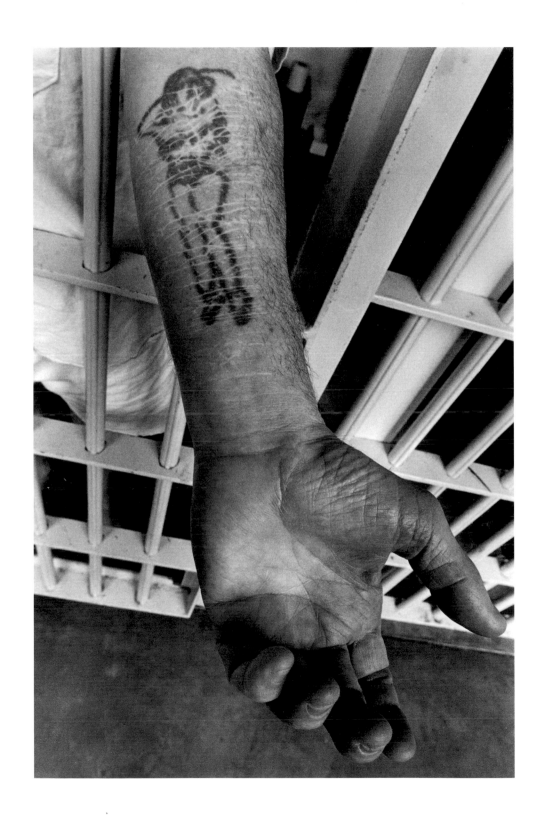

Tattoo and self-inflicted wounds

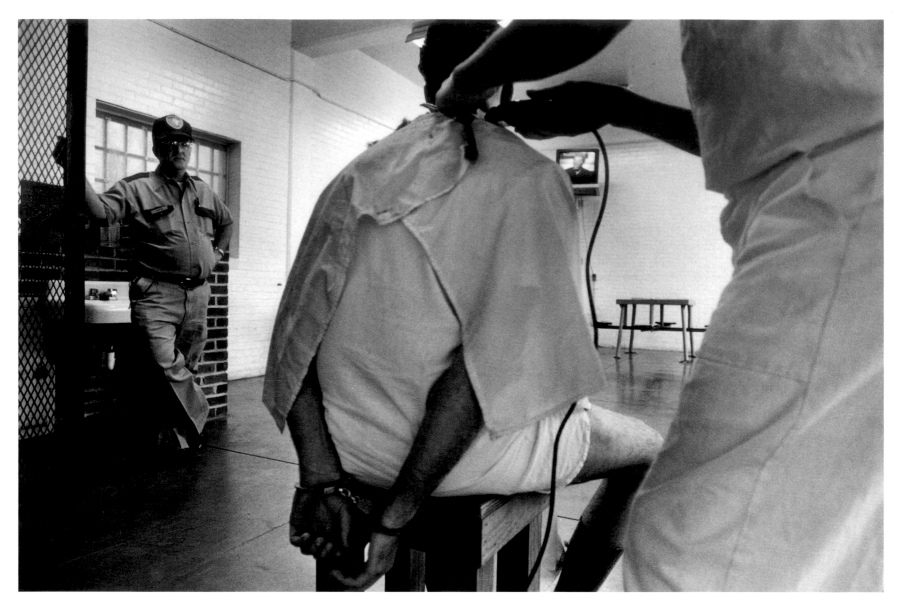

Haircut
Administrative Segregation cell block

Jimmy Jackson after his haircut
Administrative Segregation cell block

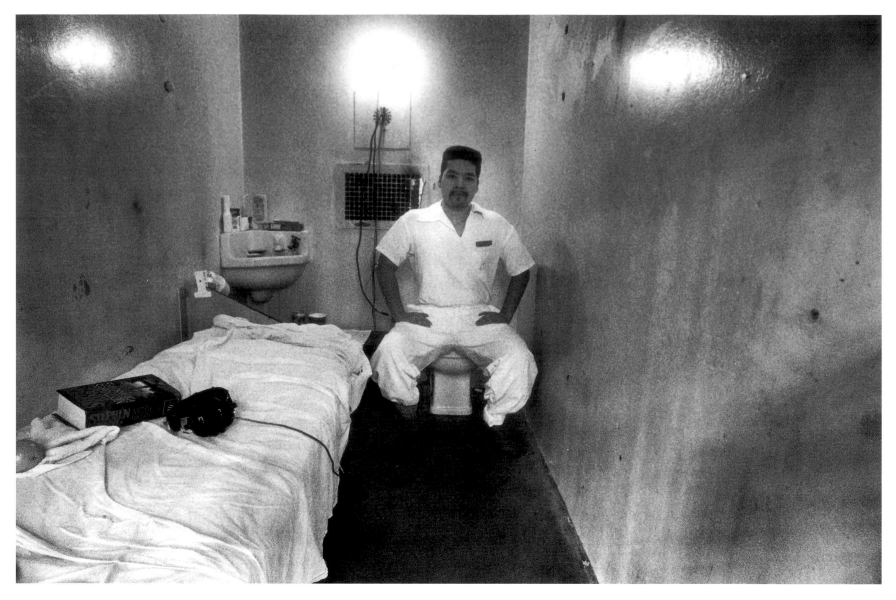

Jessy San Miguel in his "house" with Steven King's *Nightmare and Dreams*
Maximum Segregation cell block

Willie Pondexter, Jr., twenty years old
Two weeks on Death Row
Administrative Segregation cell block

I guess I'm the best hell my mother ever raised.
I was always on the wrong side of the tracks. I was never in the middle of the
tracks. I was always on this side. I saw pictures of my grandmother's people.
These were not squares. What was the norm for me?
I just started at one point and I never looked back.

Billy Mason

Name: William Michael Mason   D.R. # 999040

DOB: 1 / 30 / 54   Received: 8 / 12 / 92   Age: 38 (when rec'd)

County: Harris   Date of offense: 1 / 17 / 91

Age at time of offense: 36   Race: white   Height: 6-0

Weight: 172   Eyes: brown   Hair: brown

Native County: St. Louis   State: Missouri

Prior Occupation: tailor   Education level: 8 yrs. (GED)

Prior prison record:
TDCJ #237122, rec. 1/8/74, Harris Co., 5 yrs., theft, burglary WICT, assault to murder w/malic aforethought, discharged 9/9/76. TDCJ #279358, rec. 4/25/78, Harris Co., 55 yrs., murder, agg. robbery w/pistol, paroled to Harris Co. 12/14/90.

Summary: Convicted in the January 1991 kidnapping and murder of his wife, Deborah Ann Mason. Mrs. Mason was beaten, bound and gagged by her husband at their residence after he complained of her playing the radio too loud. He put her in the trunk of their car and drove to the San Jacinto River, where he crushed her skull with a rock. He then placed her body inside plastic garbage bags, weighted the bags with rocks, and threw her in the river. Her body was found 10 days later on the river bank.

Co-Defendants: _____

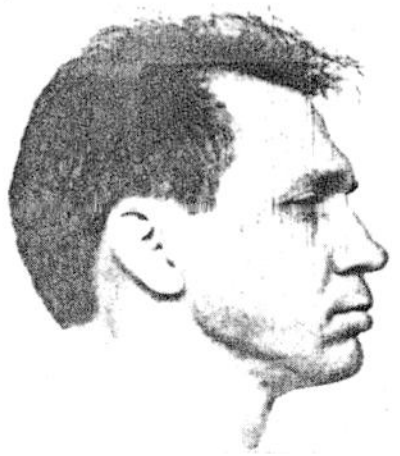

Race of Victim(s): white female

39

Billy Mason, "The Missouri Kid"
H-17 wing, row 3, cell 7, Work Capable cell block

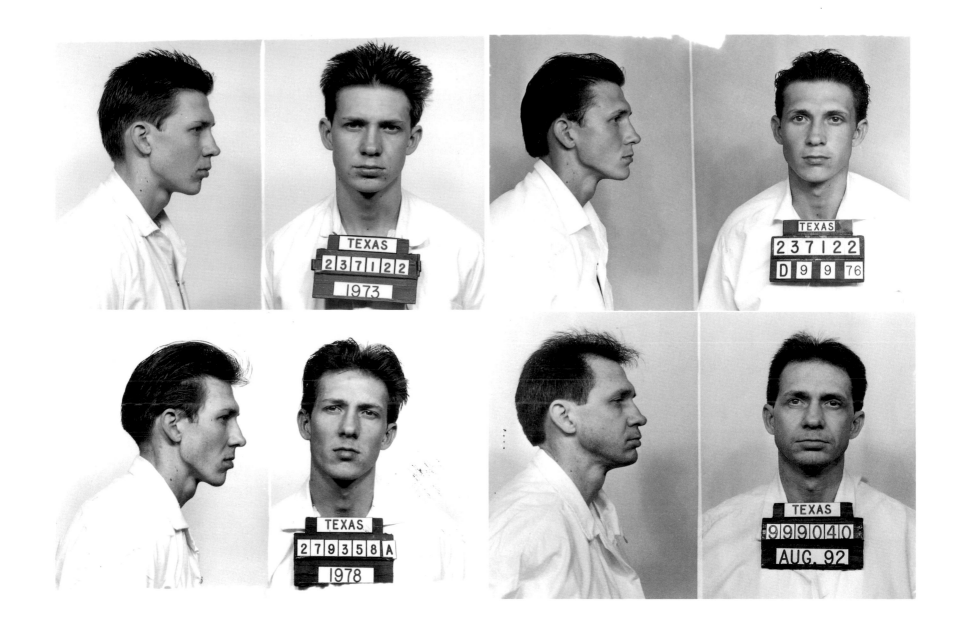

I walk in and step into the closet-sized steel-mesh cage. You're already sitting, waiting on the other side. I stand facing you while the escort uncuffs me. Arriving with shackles on no longer embarrasses me. Sometimes I think they would have us on leashes too, if they could get away with it. I never thought wearing handcuffs would become a way of life.

Martin A. Draughon,
"Never Say Goodbye—Death Row Visit"

Maximum Segregation convict being escorted to an Easter Sunday visit

Convicts' side of the visiting room
Ellis unit

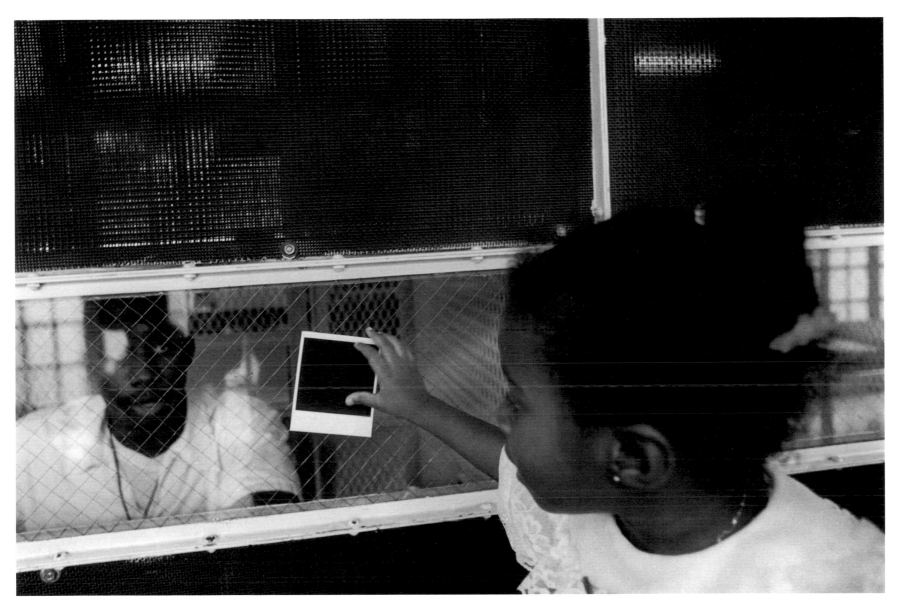

Randy visiting with his two-year-old daughter
Visiting room

Locked cage for Administrative Segregation convicts
Visiting room

Martin Draughon greeting his mother
Visiting room

Thomas Miller-El being escorted back to his
Administrative Segregation cell

Name: Thomas Joe Miller-El   D.R.# 834

DOB: 4 / 16 / 51   Received: 2 / 26 / 86   Age: 35 (when rec'd

County: Dallas   Date of Offense: 11 / 16 / 85

Age at time of offense: 34   Race: black   Height: 6-4

Weight: 150   Eyes: brown   Hair: black

Native County: St. Augustine   State: Texas

Prior Occupation: taxi cab owner   Education level: 14 years

Prior prison record:
TDC #211274, received 7-2-70 from Harris Co. with 8-year sentence for
burglary WICT and theft; paroled 11-22--74. Convicted of bank robbery
and given a 10-year federal prison term. Received at the federal
penitentiary in Terre Haute, Indiana on 7-20-76; paroled 1981.

Summary: Convicted in the November 1985 robbery-slaying of 25-year-old
Douglas Walker, a clerk at the Holdiay Inn-South in Irving. Walker and
fellow clerk Donald Ray Hall, 29, were confronted by Miller-El and his
wife, Dorothy Miller-El, and led to a back closet, where they were tied
up and shot with a 9mm automatic weapon. Walker died from his wounds and
Hall was paralyzed from the chest down. The robbers took approx. $500 in
cash and a floor safe containing approx. $2,500 in cash and coins from
the hotel at 4440 West Airport Freeway. Miller-El was arrested by Houston
police on Nov. 21, 1985. He was also given a 2-year and 5-year prison sentences in
June 1986 for a drug offenses and weapon committed in Dallas County in September 1985.
Co-Defendants: Dorothy Miller-El #432170, B/F, DOB: 4/24/48, rec. 9/23/86
with life sentence for att. capital murder and murder. Twanna Bonner Bey
#430336, W/F, DOB: 7/4/62, rec. 9-2-86, 5 yrs., att. murder (2).
Kennard Flowers, #431144, B/M, DOB: 3/6/62, rec. 9/11/06, 20 yrs., att.
Race of Victim(s): capital murder and drug offenses.

white male

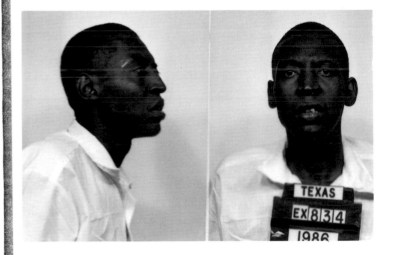

It seems as though the K.K.K., or (AKA) Good ole Boy system here in America has moved from their normal attire and into the prison system with various race and ethnic back grounds. Yet in still, it's the most sadistic, tortuous, demeaning, dehumanizing, and inhumane reflections of death and destruction known to humanity, where ever it face appears, from the Whitehouse to the Death house. It's really amazing that such sadistic methods are totally well and alive anywhere within such a high tech society. Yet this savagery is constantly growing, and is systematically a part of this Country's Politically correct methods of behavior. And very seldom noticed by the majority of the people who are being exploited I imagine. Basically, this has become more or less a complete way of life, and is molded into the minds, hearts, and spirits of our society for the most part. Even the so-called black people who are in authority have learned how to apply and enforce this dehumanizing behavior pattern upon other human Beings. Therefore, it's no longer just a race issue... it's a economical class reality.

I frequently wonder about the so-called free world, or free people, as alleged by many of my comrades. Because in reality, there is no such a thing, since most people are merely a reflection of the prison's built around them by their indoctrinated perspectives of social correctness. Much of which has been established by politically, and socially rich and powerful leaders to accommodate, employ, and exercise their purposes for greed and human domination. I'm sure that my letter will fall

light years short of adequately addressing the apparent savagery which I experience, and see daily here on death row. Nevertheless, I'm hopeful that my voice has provided some idea or thoughts to ponder. As You journey into your tomorrows beyond this slave camp, I wish You the very Best in all that You do.

Take Care Brother, before I wind up boring and / or depressing You beyond reason.

Sincerely With Love,

Thomas Miller-El
One week after a stay of execution

Feeding (Kool-Aid)
J-23 wing, Maximum Segregation cell block

Dinner tray with plastic spoon

Convict passing food
with a rolled-up newspaper
Maximum Segregation cell block

Kool-Aid, lunch
Administrative Segregation cell block

I haven't seen my real parents since the state took me away from 'em—cigarette burns, kicked down the stairs, stuff like that. They put me in adoption homes over and over. My dad died when I was in a hospital in Galveston—when I say hospital, I mean a mental hospital. I kept letting out my feelings that my people did to me on other people. Whenever I had the love and had a chance to make something out of it, I didn't know how to deal with it, you know. After my dad died they took me out of there and I got picked up for kidnapping—from there I kept going to prison, prison, prison.

Jamie McCosky

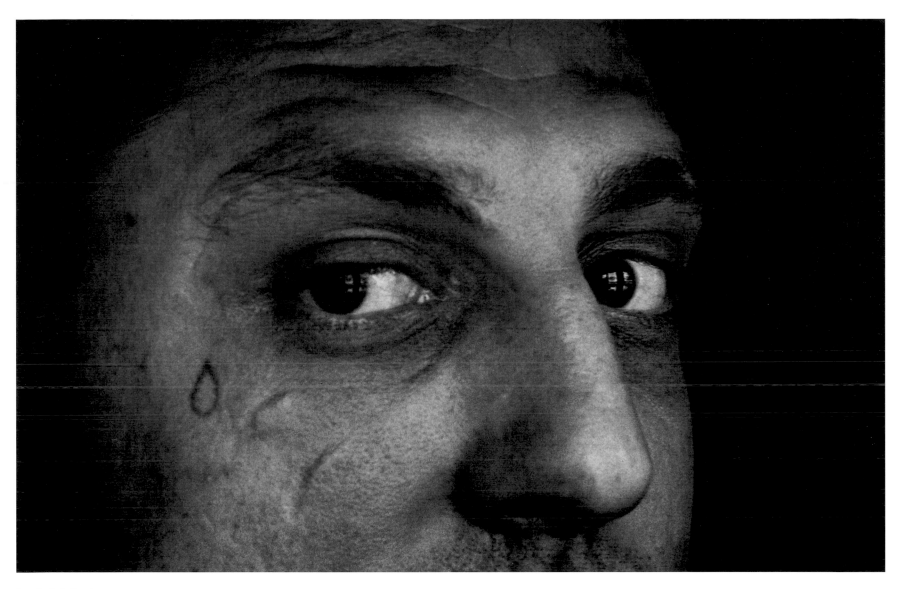

Jamie McCosky
Tattoo tear and prison scars
J-23 wing, Maximum Segregation cell block

Convict with girlie magazines
Work Capable cell block

Rocky watching TV
Work Capable dayroom

"Recreating"
Dayroom, Work Capable cell block

Convict #851
Dayroom, H-19 wing

O. J. Simpson on Death Row

Playing dominoes
Dayroom

William Kitchens, "Recreating"
J-21 wing, Maximum Segregation cell block

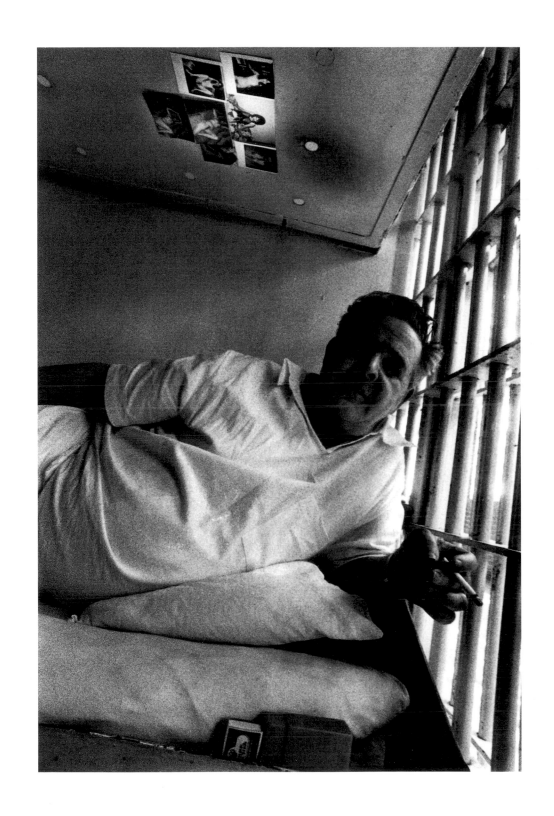

Henry Lee Lucas, serial killer
Work Capable cell block

Name: RUBEN MONTOYA CANTU   D.R.# 804

DOB: 12 / 05 / 66   Received: 09 / 10 / 85   Age: 18   (when rec'd

County: Bexar   Date of Offense: 12 / 08 / 84

Age at time of offense: 18   Race: Hispanic   Height: 5'10"

Weight: 142   Eyes: Brown   Hair: Black

Native County: Bexar   State: Texas

Prior Occupation: Laborer   Education level: 9 years

Prior prison record:
   None

Summary: Convicted of capital murder for the shooting/robbery of Pedro Gomez and

           Juan Moreno. Moreno survived the gunshot wounds and testified in the case.

           Gomez, 35, died as a result of multiple rimfire rifle wounds.

           Approximately $600 and a watch was taken.

Co-Defendants: David Garza (certified to stand trial as an adult)
   DOB: 08/10/69 (15) H/M #404297 Rec'd: 08/30/85 (16) 20-years/Robbery Bexar Co.

Race of Victim(s):   Hispanic Male

Cell wall drawing by Ruben Cantu

EXECUTED 8/24/93

I'm a religious person. I believe in God, I'm a Christian. I have a very difficult time with people who say that the death penalty is approved by God in the Bible. Yet we have all these people down here, especially in the Bible Belt, in Texas, and these people are saying the death penalty is approved by God. Christ was crucified for their sins.

David Herman

Sunday church meeting
Dayroom

Singing "Amazing Grace"
Easter Sunday

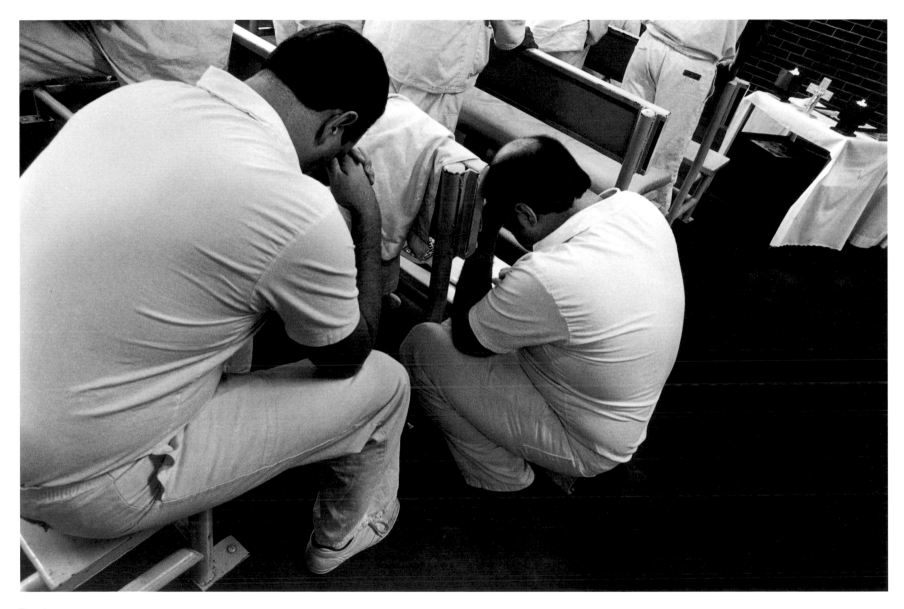

Praying
Catholic service

Baptism of Robert Anderson
Ellis chapel

A moment of prayer
Easter Sunday

Garment factory? It's a personal decision.

There's part of me not comfortable working for the state system, especially making officers' clothing. On the other hand, work is work, labor is labor, time is time. Whatever I do to pass the time . . . for the other privileges I have, it's worth it for me. I'll eat a lot of shit working for the system for my mother to not visit me in those [visiting room] cages.

James Beathard

Garment factory

Death Row Workers
Garment factory

Anibal Rousseau
Garment factory

Sewing guards' uniform pants
Garment factory

Worker
Garment factory

Paul Colella
Garment factory

Shakedown after garment factory shift

Convict with scissors
Garment factory

Guard tower seen through a hole from a bullet shot at an escaping inmate
Garment factory wall

Perry Mason on TV

Robert Tennard
Work Capable cell block

B. R. Bennett
H-19 wing, row 3, cell 11

Looking out onto the yard
Work Capable cell block

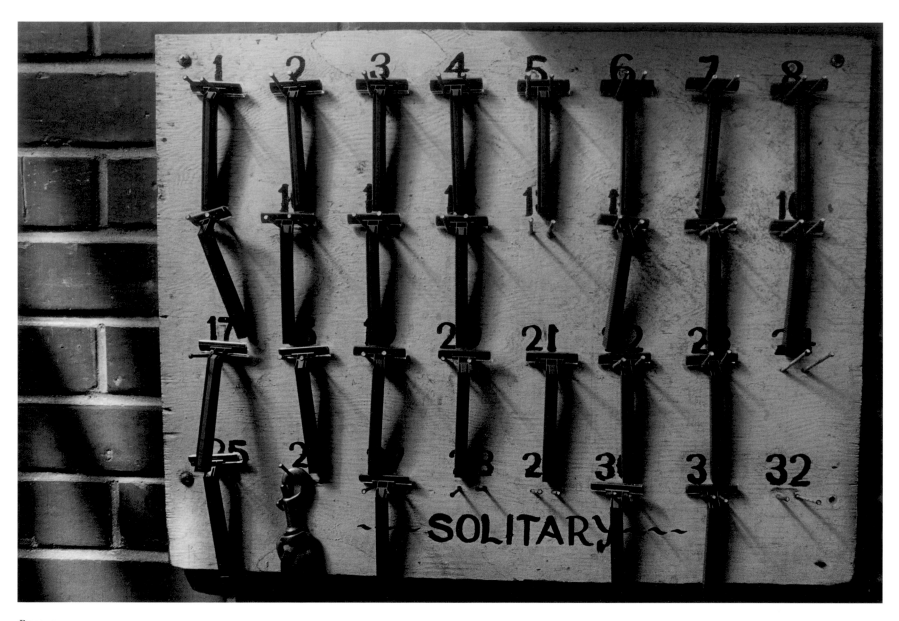

Razors
Solitary confinement

Jessy San Miguel
Single-man recreation yard
Maximum Segregation cell block

Bed count after lights out
Work Capable cell block

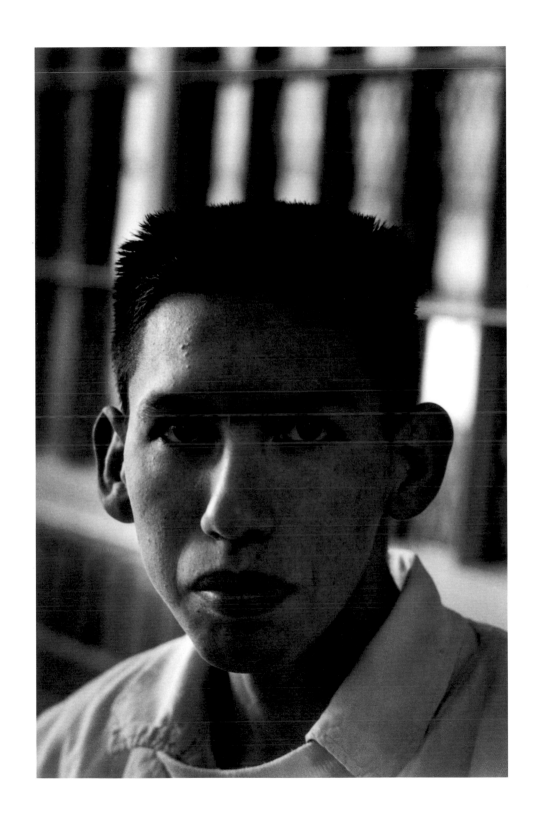

Mauro Barraza
On the Row at seventeen years old

I can see all the people in the cells [from the yard]. I see some of 'em are watching TV, some listening to the radio, some writing, some painting. There were some folks that were actually fighting demons in their cells—screaming, going crazy, beating on the walls. Folks sittin' up there just talking to each other. Folks yellin' over the wire talking about fuckin' each other in the ass.

I realized . . . this thing is so huge—it just dawned on me that there's just absolutely no way to put it in any one category. . . .

Bobby West

Weight lifter with makeshift barbells
H-20 wing, Work Capable cell block

Michael Lynn Riley,
with hand-rolled cigarette
Dayroom

94

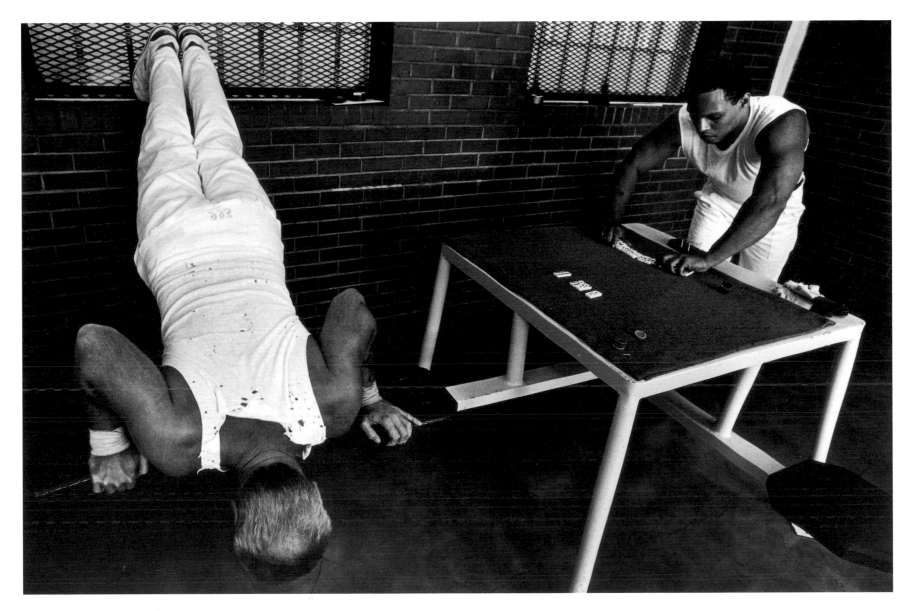

Push-ups and domino player
Dayroom

Resting on the yard

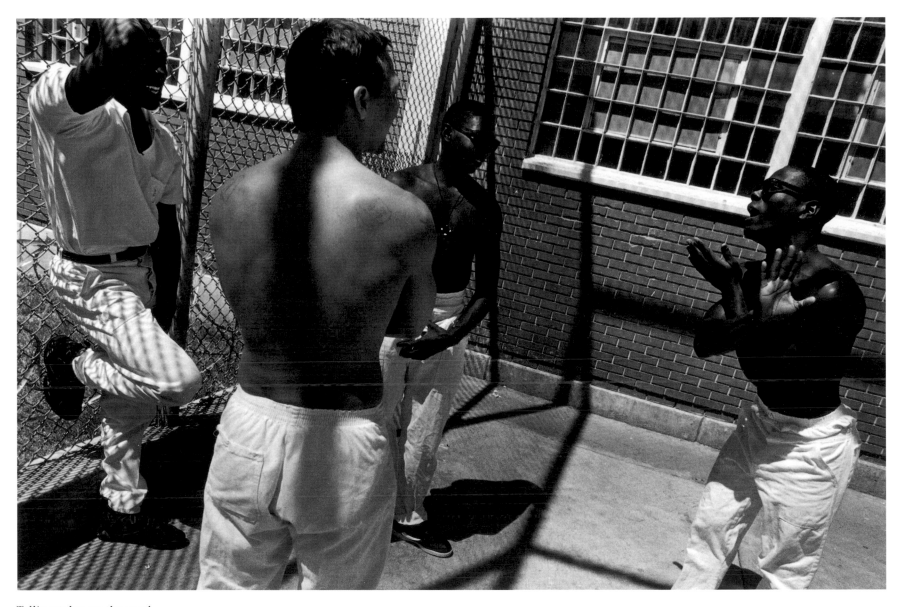

Telling tales on the yard

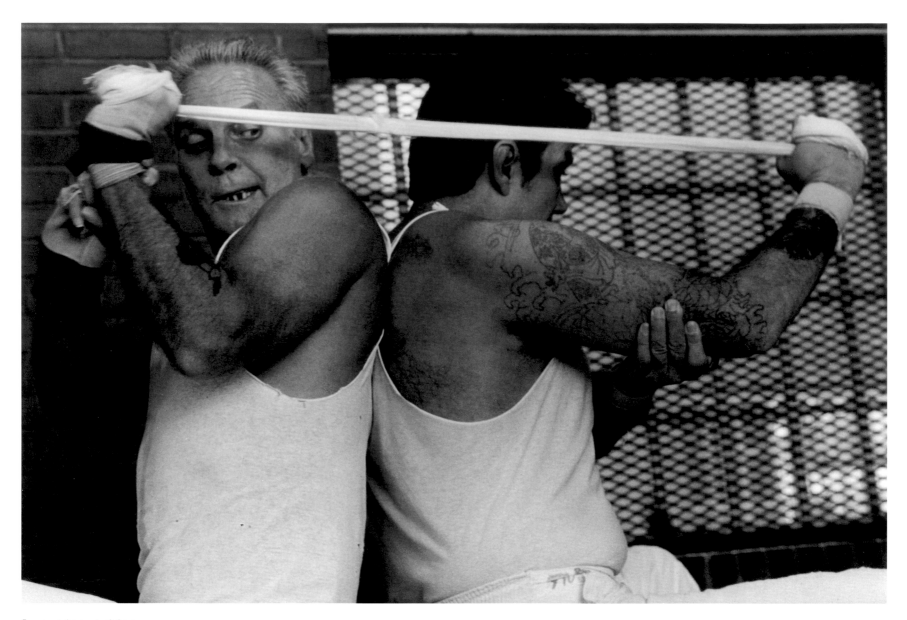

Isometric exercising
Dayroom

Handball in the yard

Walking the yard

Two convicts playing chess in single-man recreation yards
Maximum Segregation cell block

Name: Emerson Edward Rudd   D.R.# 936

DOB: 8 / 9 / 70   Received: 4 / 13 / 89   Age: 18   (when rec'd

County: Dallas   Date of Offense: 9 / 2 / 88

Age at time of offense: 18   Race: black   Height: 5-8

Weight: 145   Eyes: brown   Hair: black

Native County: Dallas   State: Texas

Prior Occupation: laborer   Education level: 11 years

Prior prison record:

    None

Summary: Convicted in the shooting death of 23-year-old Steve Morgan
during the robbery of a Captain D's Seafood restaurant in
Dallas. Rudd and three accomplices entered the restaurant at
2621 S. Westmoreland Rd. and demanded money at gunpoint. Morgan,
manager of the restaurant, was shot once in the abdomen after
handing over money from the cash register to the bandits. He
died at a Dallas hospital early the next morning. Rudd and
his accomplices were arrested two days later when their getaway
car was spotted by police. An employee who witnessed the shooting
of Morgan positively identified Rudd as the killer. Approximately
$800 was taken from restaurant in the robbery.

Co-Defendants: Darron Price, B/M, DOB: 3-29-71; Kendrick Smart, B/M,
DOB: 5-18-71; Frenchitt Collins, B/M, 2-13-70. The three were sentenced to
terms of 20 yrs., 15 yrs. and 10 yrs. respectively for murder and agg. robbery

Race of Victim(s): black male

Emerson Rudd
J-23 wing, Maximum Segregation cell block

January 3,1995

Emerson E. Rudd
#000936
Ellis One Unit
Huntsville,Texas 77343

GENERAL INMATE CORRESPONDENCE • TEXAS DEPARTMENT OF CRIMINAL JUSTICE — INSTITUTIONAL DIVISION
☆ I-290 (07/93)

My Dearest Friend,

On April 16, 1963, Dr. Martin Luther King Jr. spoke of justice in a letter from Brimingham Jail by directly referring to St. Augustine's statement that: "An unjust law is no law at all". With his keen understanding of human nature, Dr. King proclaimed that: "An unjust law is a code that is out of harmony with moral law and that a law that up-lifts human personality is--JUST... Any law that degrades human personality is-- UNJUST...

On December 27,1994. "I", "The Young Lion" received a death warrant via U.S. Postal Service from Dallas County. It read: On January 26,1995. I am to be executed-- K I L L E D ! By way of "Lethal Injection" at midnight before sunrise. The warrant took me by surprise. I was under the impression the Supreme Court had not ruled on my case. Also being I don't have any legal representation. This has more than surprised me. Its knocked me in the pit of darkness and I don't know if I'll ever be able to find the light again!

The desire for retribution against those who have been convicted of violent crimes is understandable. But these feelings poorly serve the cause of-- **J U S T I C E !** Executions seem to only add to the vicious cycle of barbarism and brutality that is consuming America's society. Knowing the state of Texas has taken out a contract on my life. Is an outrage within itself... More over, its a reminder that there is still an absence of justice in this country! Especially for those dubbed-- "LOWER CLASS CITIZENS".

Being here to experience the before's and the after's of more than sixty executions. I would like to think without being conceited. I understand the system reasonably well. With this understanding allow me to say: It is very unlikely I will be executed on January 26,1995. For I have four other levels of appeals. Still the fact remains-- It could happen! Yes, it could happen "ONLY" if something went terribly wrong. Lets hope that doesn't happen.

You may be saying to yourself-- He must be terrified! Yes,
I am... But at the present, my concern of how I shall break
this news to my mother, out weights everything else. For, how
is a "SON" suppose to tell his mother he may die in less than
30 days? I've thought to call her on the phone but decided
she deserves better. I thought about writing a letter but decided
she would read and re-read that letter until the pain would
be unthinkable. Nonetheless, I will have to break the news
some way. You know, its as if, My mother and I are on two different
planets. Yet, our planets put out the same thing-- "Cold Insensitivity".
Its a world where the sun never shines. Where our surroundings
are filled with heartaches, break-ups and let downs. I want
so bad to be held by my mother. Hearing the words-- Its All
Right! I "L O V E" You... Its hard "Suzanne". Harder than I
ever imagined. I've fallen and I can't get up! Death is looking
at me and I can't get out of its way. Nor can my friends (you)
do much to change my position. One thing you can do: Write
in an attempt to take my mind away for this strange world.
I need you more "NOW", than ever before.

    Please know that your friendship (your few letters) have
helped me more than you may ever know. I "L O V E" You! I shall
never forget you and hope you will never forget me.

    On that note, I leave as I came-- "S T R O N G"

            I Didn't Ask For It To Be Over
                    But Then Again
            I Didn't Ask For It To Begin
        For That's The Way It Is With Life
        As Some Of The Most Beautiful Days
                Come Completely By Chance
            But Even The Most Beautiful Days
            Eventually Have Their Sunset...

                    LOVE ALWAYS,

                    "THE YOUNG LION"

                        " Emerson E. Kidd "

James Allridge III and
Ronald Allridge (**EXECUTED** 6/08/95)
Brothers in adjoining cells
Administrative Segregation cell block

106

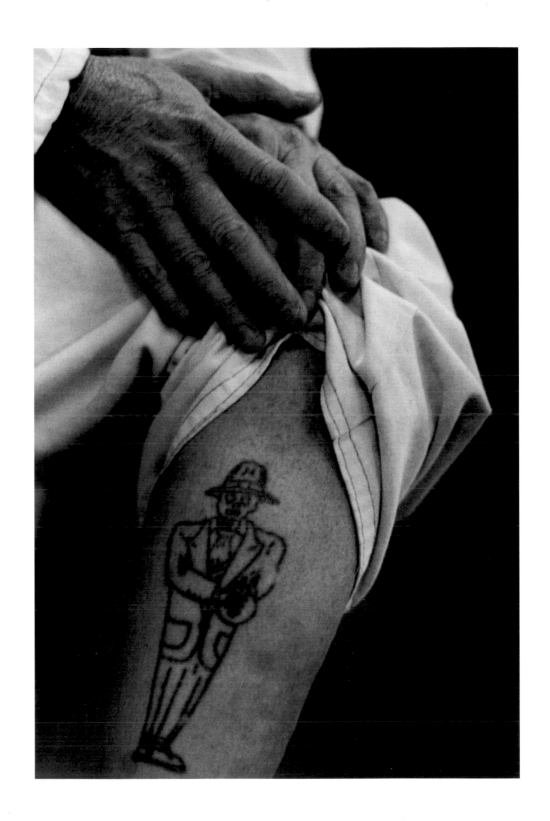

Gangster tattoo of a career criminal

Jerry Hogue
H-18 wing, row 2, cell 5

Robert Anderson
Two months on Death Row

Inmates playing chess on handmade board
Administrative Segregation cell block

Ray Kinnamon, writing a letter
EXECUTED 12/11/94

Glen McGinnis
On his twenty-first birthday

End of meal time
Administrative Segregation cell block

If my words can persuade you to discontinue this practice of executing people, please do so. If the citizens don't do away with the death penalty, Texas won't be a safe place to be. I have no revenge because hate won't solve anything.

Final words of **Raymond Carl Kinnamon,** the
last of fourteen men executed in Texas in 1994

Killer says he's ready to die
Huntsville inmate set for execution Easter night

Associated Press

HUNTSVILLE, Texas — Richard Beavers speaks calmly, laughs easily and contends that he's at peace with himself and with God.

And the convicted killer, seated in a small cage outside death row, says he's ready and looking forward to his execution Easter Sunday night for a murder in Houston in 1986.

"It's really a great day to die, to leave the body," Mr. Beavers, 38, said Wednesday. "I'm accepting responsibility for my actions, whatever the consequences may be.

"I think laying down my life is one way to apologize. I just hope the courts don't grant the rights to attorneys" to intervene.

also was shot, but she survived and testified against Mr. Beavers.

Mr. Beavers, a former neighbor accosted the couple at their Houston apartment and took them to bank machine to withdraw money so he could buy some heroin. Then he demanded that they go to the restaurant Mr. Odle managed and forced him to open the safe and turn over $6,200 in cash.

The three drove to a remote spot southeast of Houston where Mr. Beavers shot Mr. Odle, then drove to another site where he shot Mrs. Odle.

"I knew what I was doing," he said. "I knew when I knocked on that door that I would murder. I did have a hard time shooting Doug.

Name: Richard Lee Beavers   D.R.# 916

DOB: 12 / 9 / 55   Received: 10 / 18 / 88   Age: 32   (when rec'd

County: Harris   Date of Offense: 8 / 18 / 86

Age at time of offense: 30   Race: white   Height: 5-11

Weight: 200   Eyes: brown   Hair: brown

Native County: Alexander   State: Virginia

Prior Occupation: laborer   Education level: 5 years

Prior prison record:

Virginia State Prison, 10-year sentence in 1975 for armed robbery,

burglary, and abduction, paroled in 1983. While in prison, Beavers

was convicted of drug possession and escape.

Summary: Convicted in the August 1986 abduction and slaying of

Douglas G. Odle, a 24-year-old Houston restaurant manager. Odle and

his wife Jenny, also 24 at the time, were abducted from their apartment

at gunpoint and forced to drive to several banks and withdraw money from

automatic teller machines. They were then forced to drive to the restaurant

Odle managed and return with money. Beavers then forced the couple to

drive to a field in Galveston County where Doug Odle was shot through the

throat after being forced to kneel before Beavers. Beavers drove away from

the scene with Odle's wife, who was later raped, shot in the head and

left for dead. She survived a destroyed left eye and brain damage to

Co-Defendants: testify against Beavers, who was arrested by the FBI in
               Virginia following the crime.

                    No co-defendants

Race of Victim(s):   white male

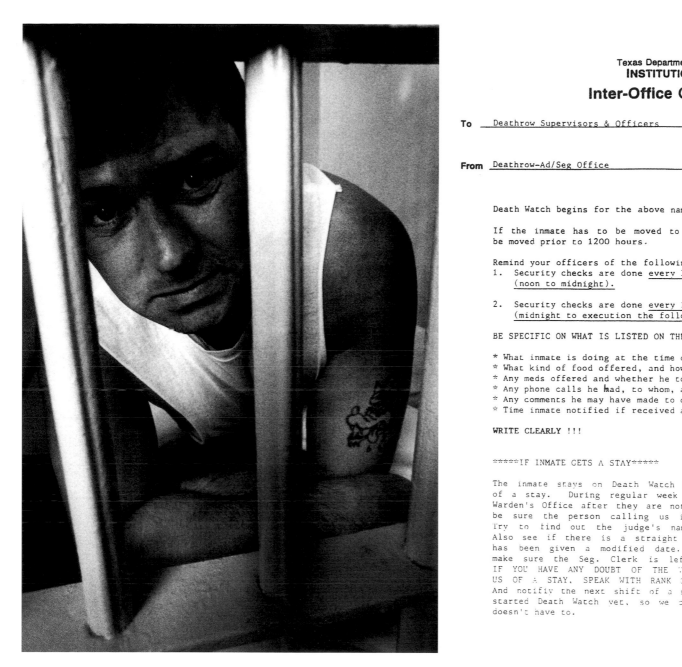

Richard Beavers a few hours before his execution
Death Watch cell

SO-4

Texas Department of Criminal Justice
INSTITUTIONAL DIVISION
Inter-Office Communications

To   <u>Deathrow Supervisors & Officers</u>   Date <u>April 2, 1994</u>

From <u>Deathrow-Ad/Seg Office</u>   Subject **DEATH WATCH**
 Beavers, Richard #916

(inmate name & TDC #)

Death Watch begins for the above named inmate at noon on <u>04/02/94</u>.

If the inmate has to be moved to the front of a D/R Seg. row, he must be moved prior to 1200 hours.

Remind your officers of the following information:
1. Security checks are done <u>every 30 minutes the first 12 hours</u> <u>(noon to midnight)</u>.

2. Security checks are done <u>every 15 minutes the last 24 hours</u> <u>(midnight to execution the following midnight)</u>.

BE SPECIFIC ON WHAT IS LISTED ON THE DEATH WATCH LOG, INCLUDE:

* What inmate is doing at the time of Security Check
* What kind of food offered, and how much he ate
* Any meds offered and whether he took them
* Any phone calls he had, to whom, and how long talked
* Any comments he may have made to officers doing Security Checks
* Time inmate notified if received a stay, this ends Death Watch

WRITE CLEARLY !!!

*****IF INMATE GETS A STAY*****

The inmate stays on Death Watch until we receive OFFICAL NOTIFICATION of a stay. During regular week day hours, we will be called by the Warden's Office after they are notified. If on weeekends or evenings, be sure the person calling us is an authorizing official of T.D.C. Try to find out the judge's name and court that issued the stay. Also see if there is a straight stay of execution, or if the inmate has been given a modified date. If he's received a modification, make sure the Seg. Clerk is left a message to update her clendar. IF YOU HAVE ANY DOUBT OF THE VALIDITY OF THE PHONE CALL NOTIFYING US OF A STAY, SPEAK WITH RANK ON DUTY BEFORE ENDING DEATH WATCH!!! And notifiy the next shift of a stay, especially if the inmate hasn't started Death Watch yet, so we don't put him in Death Watch when he doesn't have to.

HOURLY VISITS
(closed outer door)

DEATH WATCH
30 min. 1st 12 hours
15 min. last 24 hours

-

INMATE'S NAME & NUMBER   Beavers, Richard #916

HOUSING LOCATION   G 3 - 1-3

DATE	TIME	REMARKS	INITIALS
4-3-94	11:15	I/m lying on bunk	DR
4-3-94	11:30	I/m lying on bunk watching T.V.	DR
4-3-94	11:45	(I) laying on his bunk watching T.V.	VP
4-3-94	12:00	(I) standing near sink shaving	VP
4/3/94	12:15	I/m standing near door	VP
4-3-94	12:17	(I) requested and received aluminum and magnesia	VP
4-3-94	12:30	(I) walking in cell	VP
4-3-94	12:45	(I) walking in his cell	VP
4-3-94	1:00	(I) standing in his cell near door	VP
4-3-94	1:15	I/m sitting on bunk watching T.V.	DR
4-3-94	1:30	(I) laying on his bunk watching TV	VP
4-3-94	1:39	(I) talking to Sgt. Haas about visit + phone calls	VP
4-3-94	1:45	Chaplain Wilcox talking to I/m	DR
4-3-94	2:00 P.m.	I/m talking with Chaplain Wilcox	DR
4-3-94	2:15 P.m.	I/m talking with chaplain Wilcox	DR
4-3-94	2:30 P.m.	I/m out of cell for hair cut	RR
4-3-94	2:45 P.m.	I/m watching t.v. standing at door	DR
4-3-94	3:00 Pm	I/m recieved meal consisting of: Spaghetti/meat balls, corn, Pinto beans, beets, squash, cookies, garlic bread, iced punch. I/m ate some Spaghetti.	JC

SELECT STATUS

ATTACHMENT E

HOURLY VISITS
(closed outer door)

DEATH WATCH
30 min. 1st 12 hours
15 min. last 24 hours

-

INMATE'S NAME & NUMBER   Beavers, Richard #916

HOUSING LOCATION

DATE	TIME	REMARKS	INITIALS
		And one cookie.	
4-3-94	3:30 Pm	I/m standing in front of cell watching T.V.	JC
4-3-94	3:45 Pm	I/m standing in front of cell watching T.V.	JC
4-3-94	4:00 Pm	I/m requested med for from officer ___ (1-Aloaha & magnesia &1 antacid 30 cc)	RR
4-3-94	4:15 Pm	I/m sitting on bunk talking to Porter	DR
4-3-94	4:20	Log terminated for transport	

Richard Beavers being led to "the Walls" for execution
Easter Sunday, 4:20 P.M.

Richard Beavers
The last light, Easter Sunday 1994

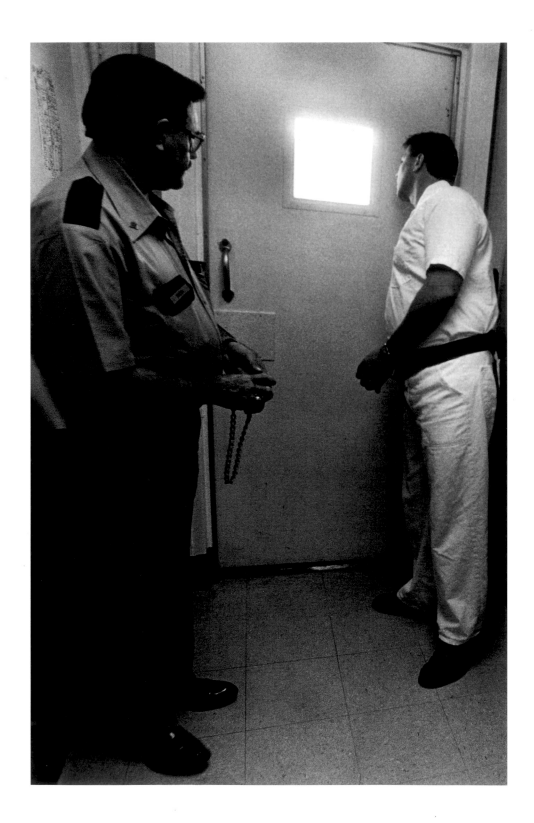

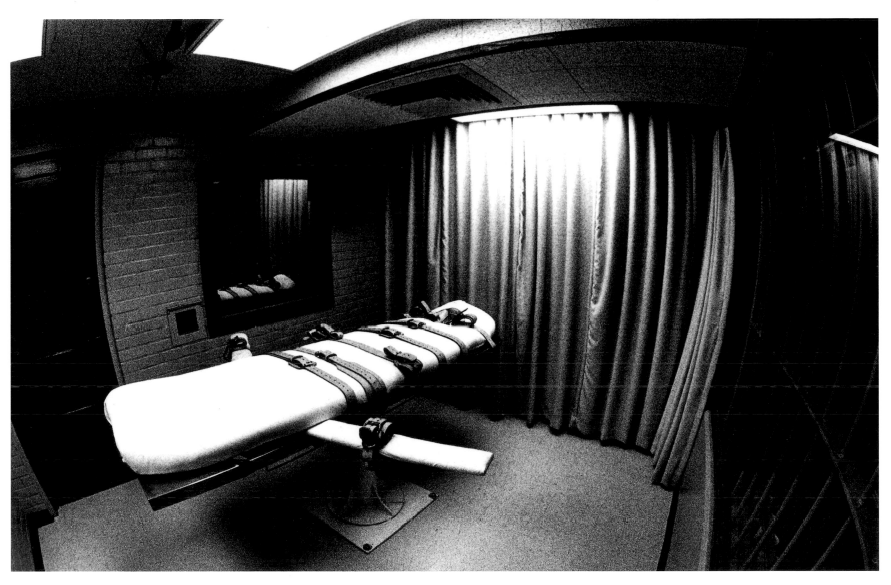

Execution chamber at "the Walls"
Huntsville, Texas

NAME: Richard Beavers #916   **EXECUTION DATE:** 04/04/94

DATE OF BIRTH: 12/09/55   **DATE RECEIVED:** 10/18/88

RACE: White   **HEIGHT:** 5'11"   **WEIGHT:** 200   **U.S. EXECUTION #:** 232

TEXAS EXECUTION #: 74   **COUNTY OF CONVICTION:** Harris

DATE OF CRIME: 08/18/86   **ESTIMATED CROWD NUMBER:** 3

ARRIVED AT THE HUNTSVILLE UNIT: 5:05 p.m.

FINAL MEAL REQUESTED: Six pieces of french toast w/syrup, jelly, butter; six barbecue spare ribs; six pieces of well-burned bacon; four scrambled eggs; five well-cooked sausage patties; french fries w/ketchup; three slices of cheese; two pieces of yellow cake with chocolate fudge icing; four cartons of milk.

TAKEN FROM HOLDING CELL: 12:08 a.m.   **SALINE SOLUTION STARTED:** 12:14 a.m.

LETHAL INJECTION GIVEN: 12:24 a.m.   **PRONOUNCED DEAD:** 12:29 a.m.

LAST STATEMENT: Jesus Christ, the way of truth and light. I thank you, Lord Jesus, for giving me the way.

A DEEPLY HIDDEN PLACE
AFTERWORD BY KEN LIGHT

Richard Beavers looks at me through the whitewashed bars of the Death Watch cell. Only hours remain before he will be led away to his execution. The cartoon-like wolf tattoo on his arm is almost ironic—he has been anything but the wolf in my conversations with him over this last day of his life. He doesn't seem capable of committing the crime for which he is about to be executed. Not that he didn't do it; in fact, he tells me he is sorry for what he did and is ready to pay the ultimate cost. As I look into his eyes, I believe he feels remorse, and I understand that he is about to be killed for something he did in another life, before Death Row.

I didn't meet Richard until my second visit to Huntsville. As I entered the prison that Easter weekend, I was escorted to the Death Row Seg office. It is small, considering that those who work there oversee more than four hundred people on the Row. Over the inner door is a hand-painted sign reading "Ignorance Is Expensive." I noticed on the large wall calendar where all the upcoming executions are listed that Richard Beavers's date was Easter Sunday. I had

been in the prison before when inmates were moved to the Death Watch cell, but they had all been given stays and were then moved back onto the Row to wait out the months or years it might take for their appeals to move through the courts. Captain West, the head officer of Death Row, reluctantly told me that Richard's execution was going to happen. I don't think he particularly wanted me to be inside the cell block while the execution process was taking place or to witness Richard being led to his death.

The news of this execution both scared and excited me. As a photographer I was feeling a deep responsibility to witness the world of Death Row. Obviously such an event   an impending execution—held the potential for powerful images. But what about the human element? How would Richard feel about allowing an outsider to make photographs of him in his last moments? I faced a dual dilemma. One was personal; I was forced to think about how I might relate to him as a subject and what my role was as witness and photographer. The other was more practical, in that the prison system required me to obtain a model release for all the

inmates I photographed. So before I could make an image of Richard I needed his consent and signature.

As I approached Richard's cell, many thoughts went through my head. I was sure that he knew of my presence, since the Death Row grapevine works fast and efficiently. An outsider with a camera doesn't go unnoticed, and I had already made many photographs, as well as numerous friends, on my first week-long visit three months earlier. Locating his cell, I approached. I explained who I was and what I was doing. He looked at me through the bars of his segregation block cell and said no, he didn't want to have his photograph taken. I stood there thinking about what to do. One part of me was saying walk away, let him be, while another was saying talk to him. I ended up spending thirty minutes looking deeply into his eyes, not blinking for the longest time, trying to describe the importance of the project and explain why I wanted to take his photograph.

I told him of Suzanne's and my premise that, once inmates are sent to Death Row, any public notion of them as persons is lost inside an unseen world. Rarely were photographers given any access other than an occasional walk-through, which really didn't allow them to see the environment or explore it with any depth of understanding: it was simply presented as an editorial illustration. I explained how it was our intention to try to see how the men on the Row created their own world and survived the years there. We wanted to find out who they were, to get beyond the mug shots that were almost always the final representation of a Death Row inmate's life.

Richard thought for a few moments about my ideas and then said yes. It was a strange sort of victory, for I knew that the man standing opposite me and signing my model release would never see the photographs.

The Death Watch cell is on the first row of G-13, one of several wings of Death Row. It is a cell not unlike others on the Row, except that it is the last stop before the inmate is moved to the chamber. The scenario there, played over and over again, seems almost routine for inmates and guards alike. This particular day happens to be Easter; the only change from the usual round of activity is that each man gets a dyed-blue hard-boiled egg, which, I am told, is a real treat. Catholic services in the day room that Sunday morning reverberate with the words of "Amazing Grace," sung because of the impending execution. That Beavers is getting the lethal injection on Easter is not lost on his fellow prisoners.

Richard sits in the Death Watch cell, waiting for his time to come. His every move, including what he eats and with whom he talks, is recorded in a special Death Watch log. As the final

hour gets closer, the activity mounts. Calls between the Death Row wing and the warden's office increase. Soon a small contingent of officers arrives, death warrant in hand. They slowly open Richard's cell and enter, then have him turn around so they can fasten a large leather belt around his waist and handcuff his hands to it. There is an almost schizophrenic feeling in the prison wing; everyone is quiet, but the air is electrified.

For his last meal, Richard has requested six pieces of french toast with syrup, jelly and butter, six barbecued spareribs, six pieces of well-burned bacon, four scrambled eggs, five well-cooked sausage patties, french fries with ketchup, three slices of cheese, two pieces of yellow cake with chocolate fudge icing, and four cartons of milk.

The moment has come. It is about 4:20 in the afternoon; Richard Beavers is leaving his home of many years and being moved to the Walls for his execution. Slowly he emerges from the Death Watch cell. He is wearing a white cotton prison uniform, the same type of clothes he has always worn over these last years. The escorts—the lieutenant in charge of Death Row that afternoon and one of the guards—slowly move him towards the locked gate of the cell block. Many of the inmates who can see this ritual taking place seem to look through the activity, pretending not to notice that anything unusual is happening.

The gate separating the Ellis population from Death Row is closed. The hall, normally alive with activity, has been cleared and is quiet. Along with a small entourage, Richard is quickly

moved toward the prison infirmary, where he will be met and taken to the Walls for his final hours.

As we enter the narrow infirmary hallway, the tension rises. The execution will actually happen—this is not a test, there will be no reprieve. In a few hours, this man staring out the window of the infirmary door of Ellis will be given a lethal injection. The place is silent. One guard holds a small bag of Richard's articles, personal items such as a toothbrush; the rest of his things have been given away to those waiting for their day to come. The other guard has a clipboard holding the official records, including the death warrant, that legitimize the state's process. We wait for the moment when the final door will open and inmate 916 will leave Ellis after eight years of life on Death Row. Richard is nervous as he looks out into the bright powerful light of Easter Sunday afternoon, the last sunlight he will see. It must seem like an eternity.

I feel as though I am in a dream. Looking through the viewfinder of my camera as all this transpires, I find it hard to imagine that this physically healthy person, on whom I am carefully focusing my lens as I click off frame after frame, will, in a few hours, no longer be on this earth.

As the interior door opens, I am struck by the almost-blinding sunlight. I realize that this is probably the first time in eight years that Richard has left the wings of Death Row. We step cautiously down some stairs out the back door of the infirmary. His legs are chained, and he moves slowly into the prison van that will drive him to his place of execution. I watch in silence, with the others, as the motor starts and the van begins to leave. It all seems surreal. Feeling dazed, I become lost in my own thoughts. I am unable to make any more photographs and retreat to my small motel room.

Later that evening, Richard Beavers's eyes stare out at me again, this time beneath the headline in a local newspaper: "Murderer Beavers slated for execution." It is a photograph I do not recognize, a mug shot taken in 1986 after his arrest for the abduction and murder of Douglas Odle and the sexual assault and shooting of Odle's wife. The robbery netted Beavers, then a heroin addict, $6,200—more than many other men on Death Row got in their robbery-murder crimes. The newspaper article, which describes how Beavers made his victim get down on his knees and then shot him in the head, says nothing of Richard's life on Death Row. It is as if the last eight years have been invisible, and I realize that this is the case for all the men entering that world.

That same night Suzanne and I stand outside the Walls in downtown Huntsville, where Richard will receive the lethal injection. There are no more than eight protesters, but they are held carefully behind yellow police line tape, as if they must be prevented from somehow storming the prison. It seems anticlimactic when the witnesses file into the prison and sometime later come out. The execution has been carried out just past midnight, minutes after the end of Easter Sunday.

It is hard to comprehend that the man I visited hours before, whose hand I shook, whom I promised that I would send his mother a last

photograph, has been killed by the state. It has all seemed so routine, so matter-of-fact.

Inmates explained to me the next day that Richard Beavers had "given it up": having found God, he felt that, to be at peace, rather than fight the execution he should go quietly and hope to gain redemption in the afterlife.

This attitude enraged many prisoners. A few of them confronted Reverend Wilcox, who was making his rounds. He had been of counsel to Richard and visited him on that last day. The men questioned whether Wilcox had in fact pressured Richard with a fundamentalism that left the condemned man nothing to do but go to his death without resistance. These inmates considered it "institutional suicide," and thought Beavers a coward; if he had wanted to die, he should have done it himself, and not jeopardize the others who were continuing to fight for their appeals.

But was Richard's choice so surprising? The experience of being locked up for years and years on Death Row alters one's sense of what is real. Even given the sometimes lengthy criminal records of the inmates, which would seem to make them hardened, they are mortals; they face the idea of death daily, and they have become institutionalized—some would say socialized—to the ways and schedules of their keepers.

It was easy sometimes, when visiting and talking to them inside their cells, to forget that every one of them had been convicted of some capital offense and in many cases murdered numerous people during the commission of a crime. It was possible to begin to see them as

humans, as those who had often had their own tragic stories before coming to Death Row. I could see how they had tried in many different ways to hold on to their humanity—I could see them laugh, be creative, find an inner spirit, dream and mourn. I always remembered, however, that in the free world there were victims—families, spouses and relatives whose lives had also been changed forever.

Entering the world of Death Row with my camera was like walking along a very thin line. Photographers are often expected to be neutral in their observations. I have in my own work rejected this notion; like many documentary photographers before me, I feel that the passionate image can and should be made in a spirit of concern about the issues surrounding a particular subject. Too often, whether because of insufficient time for a given assignment or the photographer's unwillingness to take risks, pictures turn out to be simply good illustrations with no feeling of connection to the subject.

There have been times when I have been ambivalent about those whom I have photographed, but mostly I have tried to choose subjects whose humanity I can perceive even in the most difficult of situations. Although many consider this vision of photography to be old-fashioned, I believe it is valuable in a world that seems largely to make heroes of the rich and famous. I have found that the average person has more dignity and sense of purpose than those elevated by paparazzi and the mass media.

I realized that the men I would see on Death Row had committed crimes that were often better not described. Hollywood doesn't even touch the human tragedy and suffering that has been wrought by many locked within the Ellis walls. I had myself been robbed at gunpoint years before by similarly predatory men. I knew that my beliefs would be tested by my encounters with these prisoners; I wondered whether I would be able to see the human side of their world, and whether they would trust me.

The camera has given me a way of seeing firsthand the worlds of others. Photographing Death Row would allow me to enter a place so deeply hidden that I couldn't begin to visualize what it might be like. This was an odd experience, because I am almost always conscious of the images that already exist. With each new photographic journey, I have been aware of my predecessors and colleagues, of what they have found and even how they conceptualized their work. But now my only clues were a few other projects photographers had done on prisons, and general population is a world apart from the one occupied by those awaiting execution. So I entered this process with little knowledge of what to expect. I do hold the view that the death penalty is an archaic form of justice. While I believe in justice and in paying for one's acts, I don't believe that killing, whether done by an individual or by the state apparatus, approaches a twenty-first century answer to the problem of crime.

Most photographers will tell you that part of the process is talking with your subjects, either before the shutter is released or after. I knew that, given the situation, these conversations would have an intensity that would set them apart from those associated with my other proj-

ects. Such was the case. Men on the Row are truly hungry for face-to-face encounters. Being a rare inside visitor not separated from them by the visiting room glass, I could listen intently; I could enter their cells and shake their hands. For most, because the process of talking was in the moment—in their time, Death Row time— it was more meaningful than having a photograph taken. Many thought that they might not survive to see the photos in our book, and that has turned out to be true.

I felt that my role as witness was important. I strongly believe that this is one of documentary photography's most urgent missions. Because we are bombarded with an almost unviewable series of lightning-fast cuts in TV and movies, the still image is now one of the few means by which we can take a longer look at the world as it spins past our eyes.

I believe that photographers should make every attempt to get their pictures seen in as many venues as possible. If documentary work is to succeed as witness, it must reach an audience. Sometimes the venues will be commercial and have attendant risks—perhaps only part of a body of work is seen, or the context is inappropriate, or the accompanying captions or text misrepresent the intention of a project. It is possible for the work to appear to mean something totally different from what the photographer had in mind. This has troubled me as my photographs have gone out into the world. One inmate whom I had photographed wrote to me about an image that "was used in a sleaze publication in England that accused me of being so dangerous the guards thought I would slit your throat if you got too close."

His words made me think about photographic representation. We bring so much of ourselves to the images we make. I choose the decisive moment and the camera records the interaction with my subjects in a fraction of a second. How much of that impression consists of what they think I want to see? To what extent am I limited to what they allow me to see? Have I stumbled into something that is actually representative of the real environment? I have had no sense of my own limitations and handicaps in this place called Death Row, but the more I was permitted to see and photograph the more I was able to understand. Carrying out the work over a period of weeks gave me a better opportunity to see and the inmates a chance to let me do so.

The freezing of the moment is photography's miraculous gift, one that makes it possible for me to share some of what I observed, including what I was permitted to see and what was created for my camera. It also allowed me to capture Richard Beavers gazing deeply into the last light before his execution. This photograph can create a false impression for the viewer. Let there be no illusion: Richard Beavers is no more.